Table of Contents

Practice Test #1

English

Questions 1–5 refer to the following passage:

What Is Disturbing the Fun?

It was in this apartment, also, that there stood against the western wall, a gigantic clock of ebony. Its pendulum swung to and fro with a dull, heavy, monotonous clang; and when the minute-hand made the circuit of the face, and the hour was to be stricken, there came from the brazen lungs of the clock a sound which was clear and loud and deep and exceedingly musical, but of so peculiar a note and emphasis that, at each lapse of an hour, the musicians of the orchestra were constrained to pause, momentarily, in their performance, to harken to the sound; and thus the waltzers perforce ceased their evolutions; and there was a brief disconcert of the whole gay company; and, while the chimes of the clock yet rang, it was observed that the giddiest grew pale, and the more aged and sedate passed their hands over their brows as if in confused revery or meditation. But when the echoes had fully ceased, a light laughter at once pervaded the assembly; the musicians looked at each other and smiled as if at their own nervousness and folly, and made whispering vows, each to the other, that the next chiming of the clock should produce in them no similar emotion; and then, after the lapse of sixty minutes (which embrace three thousand and six hundred seconds of the Time that flies), there came yet another chiming of the clock, and then were the same disconcert and tremulousness and meditation as before.
—Excerpted from "The Masque of the Red Death" by Edgar Allan Poe

1. The clock in this passage symbolizes
   a. the brief amount of time the orchestra played.
   b. the movement from early morning to evening.
   c. the passage of time and nearness of death.
   d. the fading beauty of all things.
   e. the lack of attention the dancers paid to the music.

2. The scene that is being described is of a
   a. concert.
   b. formal dinner.
   c. garden party.
   d. ball.

3. The action stops when
   a. the host announces dinner.
   b. the clock chimes the hour.
   c. an uninvited guest arrives.
   d. guests are asked to remove their masks.

4. What does the reader infer will happen in the story?
   a. The musicians will soon be playing for the king.
   b. The police will arrive to stop the evening's pleasures.
   c. The clock will explode at midnight.
   d. At least one person there will die.

5. Which words best describes the tone of this passage?
   a. lighthearted and sunny
   b. humorous and merry
   c. mysterious and forbidding
   d. angry and bitter

Questions 6–10 refer to the following passage:

There's a Certain Slant of Light

There's a certain slant of light,
On winter afternoons,
That oppresses, like the weight
Of cathedral tunes.

Heavenly hurt it gives us;
We can find no scar,
But internal difference
Where the meanings are.

None may teach it anything,
'Tis the seal, despair,—
An imperial affliction
Sent us of the air.

When it comes, the landscape listens,
Shadows hold their breath;
When it goes, 'tis like the distance
On the look of death.

—Emily Dickinson

6. What emotion is Dickinson describing in the poem?
    a. depression
    b. joy
    c. uncertainty
    d. surprise

7. "That oppresses, like the weight / Of cathedral tunes." is an example of the poetic device of
    a. alliteration
    b. personification
    c. simile
    d. metaphor

8. Which poetic device is used in the following lines?
"When it comes, the landscape listens, / Shadows hold their breath;"
    a. assonance
    b. personification
    c. simile
    d. metaphor

9. The season being described in the poem is
    a. solstice
    b. summer
    c. autumn
    d. winter

10. Which of the following words does NOT contribute to the mood of the poem?
    a. hurt
    b. scar
    c. despair
    d. cathedral

11. Writing, doing yoga, and _____ were her favorite activities.
    a. playing volleyball
    b. doing volleyball
    c. making volleyball
    d. volleyballing

12. Which sentence is written correctly?
    a. The student, who was caught cheating, was given detention.
    b. The student who was caught cheating was given detention.
    c. The student who was caught cheating, was given detention.
    d. The student; who was caught cheating; was given detention.

13. Which sentence is written most clearly?
    a. His neighbor's dog was walked for an allowance by the boy.
    b. The boy walked his neighbor's dog for an allowance.
    c. For an allowance, the boy walked the dog of his neighbor's.
    d. The dog of his neighbor's was walked by the boy for an allowance.

14. Every kid in the neighborhood has _____ own bicycle.
    a. its
    b. their
    c. our
    d. her

15. Maria thinks it is unfair that she has to _____ with her younger brother's whining all the time.
    a. put up
    b. put down
    c. put in
    d. put off

16. Enrique will _____ harder as the date of the test draws nearer.
    a. studying
    b. have studied
    c. studyed
    d. study

17. Suzanna replied _____ to her sister's plea to help her with her finances.
    a. sympathelly
    b. sympathetically
    c. sympathetilly
    d. sympathetic

18. A team of scientists _____ studying a new species of frog never found before.
    a. is
    b. are
    c. were
    d. have

19. Everyone we invited to the party _____, so it was a huge success!
    a. shown up
    b. showed up
    c. showed upped
    d. shows up

- 6 -

Identify the misspelled word in the sentences below.

20. Rudy beleives you should focus on your children more than on your marriage, due to the complexities of young minds.
    a. beleives
    b. focus
    c. complexities
    d. marriage

21. Buying prescents for others is not the most authentic way to develop new friendships.
    a. buying
    b. prescents
    c. authentic
    d. friendships

22. Raymond feels children misbehave too much, that parents have lost their athourity, and that they need to emphasize discipline more.
    a. misbehave
    b. emphasize
    c. discipline
    d. athourity

23. Larry travelled to India to participate in a pilgrimage across the Indian countryside hoping to relinquish all stress and achieve peace.
    a. travelled
    b. pilgrimage
    c. relinquish
    d. achieve

Choose the meaning of the underlined words in the sentences below.

24. The group hiked along a precipitous slope that many found unnerving.
    a. rugged
    b. dangerous
    c. steep
    d. wet

25. Saline is taking a philosophy class but finds most of the readings to be very obscure, so she has not benefited much from them.
    a. opinionated
    b. unclear
    c. offensive
    d. benign

26. As a young boy, Dorian was remiss about his homework and failed to get good grades in school.
    a. timely
    b. diligent
    c. negligent
    d. meticulous

Read the set of directions below to answer questions 27-30.

> This formula is for people with deficiencies and anemic conditions. It aids in the body's absorption of vital minerals such as iron, calcium, zinc, potassium, and sulfur. Take the following ingredients:
>
> Parsley root   Comfrey root
> Yellow dock   Watercress
> Nettles   Kelp
> Irish moss
>
> Slowly simmer equal parts of these herbs with four ounces to a half-quart of water. Continue to simmer slowly until the volume of liquid is reduced by half. Strain, reserve the liquid, and cover the herbs with water once more. Then simmer again for 10 minutes. Strain and combine the two liquids. Cook the liquid down until the volume is reduced by half. Add an equal amount of blackstrap molasses. Take one tablespoon four to five times daily, not exceeding four tablespoons in a 24-hour period.

27. What is the main reason for taking this formula?
    a. to serve as a mineral supplement
    b. to get rid of unnecessary minerals
    c. to reduce the absorption of minerals
    d. to increase the absorption of minerals

28. If a ¼ ounce of yellow dock is used, how much watercress should be used?
    a. ½ ounce
    b. ¼ ounce
    c. ? ounce
    d. 1 ounce

29. If a patient follows the directions correctly, how often could the medicine be taken?
    a. once every two hours
    b. once every four hours
    c. once every three hours
    d. once every six hours

30. Which cooking process is not required to make this formula?
    a. evaporating
    b. filtering
    c. whisking
    d. mixing

Answer questions 31 – 35 based on the debate below.

Forest Manager: Salvage logging is the removal of dead or dying forest stands left behind by a fire or disease. It has been practiced for several decades. Dead or dying trees become fuel that feeds future fires. The best way to minimize the risk of forest fires is to remove the dead timber from the forest floor. Salvage logging followed by replanting ensures the reestablishment of desirable tree species. For instance, planting conifers accelerates the return of fire resistant forests. Harvesting timber benefits forests by reducing fuel load, thinning the forest stands, and relieving competition between trees. Burned landscapes leave behind black surfaces and ash layers that result in very high soil temperatures. These high soil temperatures can kill many plant species. Logging mixes the soil, thereby decreasing surface temperatures to more normal levels. Shade from small, woody material left behind by logging also helps to decrease surface temperatures. After an area has been salvage logged, seedlings in the area begin to regenerate almost immediately; nonetheless, regeneration can take several years in unmanaged areas.

Ecology professor: Salvage logging transfers material like small, broken branches to the forest floor where it is available for fuel. The removal of larger, less flammable trees while leaving behind small dead limbs increases the risk of forest fires. In unmanaged areas, these woody materials are found more commonly on the tops of trees where they are unavailable to fires. Logging destroys old growth forests more resistant to wildfires and creates younger forests more vulnerable to severe fires. In old growth forests, branches of bigger trees are higher above the floor where fires may not reach. Replanting after wildfires creates monoculture plantations in which only a single crop is planted and produced. This monoculture creates less biological diversity and less disease resistant vegetation that in turn increases vulnerability to fire. Salvage logging also interferes with natural forest regeneration by killing most of the seedlings that reemerge on their own after a wildfire. It disrupts the soil, increases erosion, and removes most of the shade needed for young seedlings to grow.

31. According to the professor, how are unmanaged areas advantageous in distributing small, woody materials after a fire?
    a. They are left on the forest floor and provide nutrients to the soil.
    b. They are left on the forest floor and serve as fuel for fires.
    c. They are left on the tops of trees where fires cannot reach.
    d. They are distributed more evenly across the forest floor.

32. A study compared two plots of land that were managed differently after a fire. Plot A was salvage logged, while Plot B was left unmanaged. When a second fire occurred, they compared two plant groups between Plots A and B and found that both plant groups burned with greater severity in Plot A than in Plot B. Which viewpoint do these results support?
    a. only the manager
    b. only the professor
    c. both the manager and professor
    d. neither the manager nor the professor

33. What is the main idea of the forest manager's argument?
    a. Salvage logging is beneficial because it removes dead or dying timber from the forest floor, thereby reducing the risk of future fires.
    b. Salvage logging is beneficial because it has been practiced for several decades.
    c. Salvage logging is harmful because it raises soil temperatures above normal levels and threatens the health of plant species.
    d. Salvage logging is beneficial because it provides shade for seedlings to grow after a wildfire.

34. According to the professor, young forests are more vulnerable to severe fires than old growth forests. Which of the following statements does not support this view?
    a. In younger forests, small branches are closer to the forest floor and more available for fires.
    b. Old growth forests contain larger and taller trees, where branches are high up and fires may not reach.
    c. Younger forests have less biological diversity and less disease-resistant trees.
    d. Larger trees common in old growth forests serve as the main fuel source for severe fires.

35. Whose viewpoints would be validated by a future study looking at the distribution and regeneration of seedlings for several years following a wildfire in both managed and unmanaged forests?
    a. only the manager
    b. only the professor
    c. both the manager and professor
    d. neither the manager nor professor

Use the passage below to answer questions 36-40.

During the 1800s, Charles Darwin became known for his studies of plants and animals on the Galapagos Islands. He is often referred to as "the father of evolution," because he was first to describe a mechanism by which organisms change over time.

The Galapagos Islands are situated off the coast of South America. Much of Darwin's work on the islands focused on the birds. He noticed that island birds looked similar to finches on the South American continent and resembled a type of modified finch. The only differences in the finches Darwin saw were in their beaks and the kind of food they ate. Finches on the mainland were seed-eating birds, but the island finches ate insects, seeds, plant matter, egg yolks, and blood.

Darwin theorized that the island finches were offspring of one type of mainland finch. The population of finches was changing over time due to their environment. He believed the finches' eating habits changed because of the island's limited food supply. As the finches began to eat differently, the way their beaks worked and looked changed as well. For instance, insect-eating finches needed longer beaks for digging in the ground. Seed-eating and nut-eating finches required thicker beaks to crack the seed shells.

The process by which the finches changed happened over many generations. Among the population of beetle-eating finches, those finches born with longer, sharper beaks naturally had access to more beetles than those finches with shorter beaks. As a result, the sharp-beaked, insect-eating finches thrived and produced many offspring, while the short-beaked insect-eating finches gradually died out. The sharp beak was in effect selected by nature to thrive. The same thing happened in each finch population until finches within the same population began to look similar to each other and different from finches of other populations. These observations eventually led Darwin to develop the theory of natural selection.

36. Why is Charles Darwin called "the father of evolution?"
    a. because he coined the term "evolution"
    b. because he was the first scientist to study species on the Galapagos Islands
    c. because he was the first to describe how organisms changed over time
    d. because he was the first to suggest that birds adapted to their environment

37. What is the main point of this passage?
    a. to inform
    b. to entertain
    c. to critique
    d. to persuade

38. According to the passage, why did finches with sharp, long beaks thrive while other finches died off?
    a. They were able to reproduce faster than other types of finches on the island.
    b. They were more numerous and eventually outlived the other finches on the island.
    c. They were randomly selected by nature to reproduce over other types of finches on the island.
    d. They had better access to insects than other types of finches on the island.

39. Based on Darwin's studies on the islands, what could also be inferred about how geography affects the diversity of species?
    a. Geographical barriers decrease diversity of a species.
    b. Geographical barriers increase diversity of a species.
    c. Geographical barriers have an insignificant impact on the diversity of a species.
    d. There is no relationship between geographical barriers and the diversity of a species.

40. Which of the following statements correctly compares the finches Darwin observed in the Galapagos Islands with the finches found on the mainland?
    a. The island finches were very similar with no visible differences.
    b. The island finches differed only in the shape of their beaks.
    c. The island finches differed only in size.
    d. The island finches differed in the shape of their beaks and their diet.

Writing Prompt

There is at present a heated debate over the role of the United States in foreign affairs. Some experts argue that the cost and unintended consequences of American intervention are so great that the United States should simply mind its own business. Others assert that America's economic and political power necessitate foreign intervention, both to protect American interests and human rights. Another group derides these opposing views as condescending to the people of other countries, and suggests that the United States consult with foreign countries before becoming involved in their affairs.

In an organized, coherent, and supported essay explain what you think the United States should do and why it should do so. Address the pros and cons.

Mathematics

1. Restaurant customers tip their server only 8 percent for poor service. If their tip was $3.70, how much was their bill?
    a. $40.15
    b. $44.60
    c. $46.25
    d. $50.45

2. If Leonard bought 2 packs of batteries for x amount of dollars, how many packs of batteries could he purchase for $5.00 at the same rate?
    a. 10x
    b. 2/x
    c. 2x
    d. 10/x

3. Choose the algebraic expression that best represents the following situation: Jeral's test score (J) was 5 points higher than half of Kara's test score (K).
    a. $J = K/2 + 5$
    b. $J = 2K - 5$
    c. $K = (J - 1/2) - 5$
    d. $K = J/2 - 5$

4. What does $(4x - y) + (-10 + y)$ equal if $x = 3$ and $y = 4$?
    a. 2
    b. -2
    c. 22
    d. 14

5. A pasta salad was chilled in the refrigerator at 35° F overnight for 9 hours. The temperature of the pasta dish dropped from 86° F to 38° F. What was the average rate of cooling per hour?
    a. 4.8°/hr
    b. 5.3°/hr
    c. 5.15°/hr
    d. 0.532°/hr

6. Loral received all her grades for the semester (in parentheses) along with the weight for each grade, shown below. What is her final grade?

    <u>Weight</u>
        45% = 3 tests (80%, 75%, 92%)
        25% = final (88%)
        15% = paper (91%)
        15% = 2 oral quizzes each worth 25 points (22, 19)

    a. 88
    b. 86
    c. 79
    d. 85

7. What is the missing number in the sequence: 4, 6, 10, 18, ___, 66.
    a. 22
    b. 34
    c. 45
    d. 54

8. Convert 250 centimeters to kilometers.
    a. 0.0025 km
    b. 0.025 km
    c. 0.250 km
    d. 2.50 km

9. Rick renovated his home. He made his bedroom 40% larger (length and width) than its original size. If the original dimensions were 144 inches by 168 inches, how big is his room now if measured in feet?
    a. 12 ft x 14 ft
    b. 16.8 ft x 19.6 ft
    c. 4.8 ft x 5.6 ft
    d. 201.6 ft x 235.2 ft

10. What is $(x^2)^3 \cdot (y^2)^5 \cdot (y^4)^3$?
    a. $x^6 y^{22}$
    b. $x^6 y^{120}$
    c. $x^5 y^{14}$
    d. $x^6 y^{-2}$

11. Simplify the following fraction: $[(x^2)^5 y^6 z^2] / [x^4 (y^3)^4 z^2]$.
    a. $x^{40} y^{72} z^4$
    b. $x^6 y^{-6}$
    c. $x^3 y^{-1}$
    d. $x^{14} y^{18} z^4$

12. A house is 25 feet tall and a ladder is set up 35 feet away from the side of the house. Approximately how long is the ladder from the ground to the roof of the house?

    a. 43 ft

    b. 25 ft

    c. 50 ft

    d. 62 ft

13. A soda company is testing a new sized can to put on the market. The new can is 6 inches in diameter and 12 inches in height. What is the volume of the can in cubic inches?

    a. 339

    b. 113

    c. 432

    d. 226

14. A rectangular garden has a perimeter of 600 yards. If the length of the garden is 250 yards, what is the garden's width in yards?

    a. 25

    b. 50

    c. 175

    d. 350

15. Tony has the following number of T-shirts in his closet:

    White - 5

    Black - 2

    Blue - 1

    Yellow - 3

    If Tony's electricity goes out, how many T-shirts would he have to pull out of his closet to make sure he has a yellow T-shirt?

    a. 4

    b. 8

    c. 9

    d. 11

16.

y	-4	31	4	68	12
x	-2	3	0	4	2

Which of the following equations satisfies the five pairs of numbers shown in the above table?

a. $y = 2x^2 + 7$

b. $y = x^3 + 4$

c. $y = 2x$

d. $y = 3x + 1$

17. In a rectangular *x,y* coordinate system, what is the intersection of two lines formed by the equations $y = 2x + 3$ and $y = x - 5$?
    a. (5, 3)
    b. (8, 13)
    c. (-4, 13)
    d. (-8, -13)

18. A function *f(x)* is defined by $f(x) = 2x^2 + 7$. What is the value of $2f(x) - 3$?
    a. $4x^2 + 11$
    b. $4x^4 + 11$
    c. $x^2 + 11$
    d. $4x^2 + 14$

19. John buys 100 shares of stock at $100 per share. The price goes up by 10% and he sells 50 shares. Then, prices drop by 10% and he sells his remaining 50 shares. How much did he get for the last 50?
    a. $5000
    b. $5500
    c. $4900
    d. $4950

20. The lengths of the sides of a triangle are integer values. Two sides are 4 and 6 units long, respectively; what is the minimum value for the triangle's perimeter?
    a. 10 units
    b. 11 units
    c. 12 units
    d. 13 units

21. The two shortest sides of a right triangle are 6 and 8 units long, respectively. What is the length of the perimeter?
    a. 10 units
    b. 18 units
    c. 24 units
    d. 14 units

22. What is the area of an isosceles triangle inscribed in a circle of radius *r* if the base of the triangle is the diameter of the circle?
    a. r^2
    b. $2r^2$
    c. πr^2
    d. $2\pi r$

23. A regular deck of cards has 52 cards. What is the probability of drawing three aces in a row?
    a. 1 in 52
    b. 1 in 156
    c. 1 in 2000
    d. 1 in 5525

24. If p and n are positive consecutive integers such that $p > n$, and $p + n = 15$, what is the value of n?
    a. 5
    b. 6
    c. 7
    d. 8

25. What is the area of a square inscribed in a circle of radius r?
    a. r^2
    b. $2r^2$
    c. $2r^3$
    d. $2\pi r$

26. If x and y are positive integers, which of the following expressions is equivalent to $(xy)^{7y} - (xy)^y$?
    a. $(xy)^{6y}$
    b. $(xy)^{7y-1}$
    c. $(xy)^y [(xy)^7 - 1]$
    d. $(xy)^y [(xy)^{6y} - 1]$

27. The average of 3 numbers x, y, and z is 23. The average of three numbers a, b, and c is also 23. What is the average of all six numbers a, b, c, x, y, and z?
    a. 11.5
    b. 23
    c. 34.5
    d. 46

28. Which equation is represented by the graph shown below?

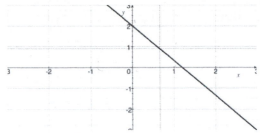

a. $y = \frac{5}{3}x + 2$

b. $y = -\frac{5}{3}x - 2$

c. $y = -\frac{5}{3}x + 2$

d. $y = \frac{5}{3}x - 2$

29. Determine the volume of a rectangular box with a length of 5 inches, a height of 7 inches, and a width of 9 inches.
    a. 445.095 in³
    b. 315 in³
    c. 45 in³
    d. 35 in³

30. A water sprinkler covers a circular area with a radius of 6 feet. If the water pressure is increased so that the radius increases to 8 feet, by approximately how much is the area covered by the water increased?
    a. 2 square feet
    b. 4 square feet
    c. 36 square feet
    d. 88 square feet

31. If $ax^2 + by = 0$, which of the following must be true?
    a. $ax^2 = by$
    b. $ax^2 = \sqrt{by}$
    c. $ax = b\sqrt{y}$
    d. $ax^2 = -by$

32. A satellite in a circular orbit rotates around the Earth every 120 minutes. If the Earth's radius is 4000 miles at sea level, and the satellite's orbit is 400 miles above sea level, approximately what distance does the satellite travel in 40 minutes?
    a. 1400 miles
    b. 9210 miles
    c. 4400 miles
    d. 4120 miles

33. Which of the following equations best describes the straight line in the graph below? Note that *a* and *b* are non-zero constants.

    a. $y = x$
    b. $x = a$
    c. $y = ax + b$
    d. $y = b$

34. A ticket agency finds that demand for tickets for a concert in a 25,000-seat stadium falls if the price is raised. The number of tickets sold, *N*, varies with the dollar price, *p*, according to the relationship $N = 25000 - 0.1p^2$. What is the lowest price at which they will sell no tickets at all?
    a. $10
    b. $25
    c. $50
    d. $500

35. Refer to the equation in Question 34, which gives the relationship between ticket price and number of tickets sold. No matter how many tickets are sold, the cost of putting on the concert is $500,000. Which of the following equations can be used to calculate the profit *Q* made for any ticket price?
    a. $Q = 25,000p - 0.1p^3$
    b. $Q = 25,000p - 0.1p^3 - 500,000$
    c. $Q = 25,000p - 0.1p^3 - 500,000p$
    d. $Q = p(25,000 - 0.1p) - 500,000$

36. For the number set {7, 12, 5, 16, 23, 44, 18, 9, Z}, which of the following values could be equal to Z if Z is the median of the set?
    a. 14
    b. 11
    c. 19
    d. 17

37. If Q is divisible by 2 and 7, which of the following is also divisible by 2 and 7?
    a. $Q + 2$
    b. $Q + 7$
    c. $Q + 28$
    d. $Q + 9$

38. Of the following expressions, which is equal to $6\sqrt{10}$?
    a. 36
    b. $\sqrt{600}$
    c. $\sqrt{360}$
    d. $\sqrt{6}$

39. Given the triangle shown in the figure, what is the length of the side A?

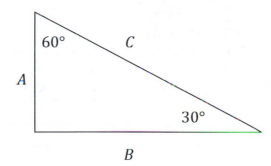

    a. $C/2$
    b. $A/2$
    c. $(A+C)/2$
    d. $2A$

40. If the two lines $2x + y = 0$ and $y = 3$ are plotted on a typical x,y coordinate grid, at which point will they intersect?
    a. -1.5, 3
    b. 1.5, 3
    c. -1.5, 0
    d. 4, 1

Science

1. A normal human sperm must contain:
    a. An X chromosome
    b. A Y chromosome
    c. 23 chromosomes
    d. B and C

Questions 2 and 3 are based upon the following figure and text:

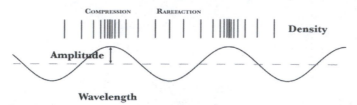

A vibrating source will produce sound by alternately forcing the air molecules in front of it closer together as it moves towards them, and then further apart as it draws away from them. In this way, alternating regions of high and low pressure, called compressions and refractions, are produced. The figure shows a typical sound wave. The volume of the sound corresponds to the magnitude of the compression, represented by the amplitude of the wave. The sound's pitch corresponds to the wave's frequency, the distance between successive compressions. Humans can hear sounds with frequencies between 20 and 20,000 Hertz. Sound waves propagate in all directions from their source. The speeds at which sound waves travel depend upon the medium they are traveling through. In dry air, sound travels at 330 m/sec at 0°C. It travels 4 times faster through water, and 15 times faster through a steel rod.

2. The sound produced by a drum is much louder and lower pitched than that produced by a bell. Which of the following statements is true about the sound wave produced by a drum compared to that produced by a bell?
    a. The amplitude is greater and the wavelength is shorter.
    b. The amplitude is greater and the wavelength is longer.
    c. The amplitude is smaller and the wavelength is longer.
    d. The amplitude is smaller and the wavelength is shorter.

3. Two sound waves of exactly the same frequency and amplitude are produced by sources that are in precisely the same position. If the sound waves are out of phase by one-half a wavelength, what will be heard by an observer standing a short distance away?

    a. A sound twice as loud as either individual signal
    b. A sound at twice the frequency of either individual signal
    c. A sound at twice the wavelength as either individual signal
    d. A sound with varying intensity

4. Which of the following animals displays the greatest fitness?
    a. A male wolf that dies young but has 4 cubs that are raised by an unrelated female
    b. A female wolf that has 3 cubs and lives to be quite old
    c. A male wolf that lives to old age and has 1 cub
    d. A female wolf that dies young after raising 3 cubs

Questions 5-10 are based upon the following figure, table, and text:
Protein Synthesis

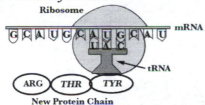

The Genetic Code

First	Codon	AA	Codon	AA	Codon	AA	Codon	AA
T	TTT	Phenylalanine	TCT	Serine	TAT	Tyrosine	TGT	Cysteine
	TTC	Phenylalanine	TCC	Serine	TAC	Tyrosine	TGC	Cysteine
	TTA	Leucine	TCA	Serine	TAA	STOP	TGA	STOP
	TTG	Leucine	TCG	Serine	TAG	STOP	TGG	Tryptophane
C	CTT	Leucine	CCT	Proline	CAT	Histidine	CGT	Arginine
	CTC	Leucine	CCC	Proline	CAC	Histidine	CGC	Arginine
	CTA	Leucine	CCA	Proline	CAA	Glycine	CGA	Arginine
	CTG	Leucine	CCG	Proline	CAG	Glycine	CGG	Arginine
A	ATT	Isoleucine	ACT	Threonine	AAT	Asparagine	AGT	Serine
	ATC	Isoleucine	ACC	Threonine	AAC	Asparagine	AGC	Serine
	ATA	Isoleucine	ACA	Threonine	AAA	Lysine	AGA	Arginine
	ATG	Methionine (START)	ACG	Threonine	AAG	Lysine	AGG	Arginine
G	GTT	Valine	GCT	Alanine	GAT	Aspartate	GGT	Glycine
	GTC	Valine	GCC	Alanine	GAC	Aspartate	GGC	Glycine
	GTA	Valine	GCA	Alanine	GAA	Glutamate	GGA	Glycine
	GTG	Valine	GCG	Alanine	GAG	Glutamate	GGG	Glycine

The genetic information for making different kinds of proteins is stored in segments of DNA molecules called genes. DNA is a chain of phosphoribose molecules containing the bases guanine (G), cytosine (C), alanine (A), and thymine (T). Each amino acid component of the protein chain is represented in the DNA by a trio of bases called a codon. This provides a code, which the cell can use to translate DNA into protein. The code, which is shown in the table, contains special codons for starting a protein chain (these chains always begin with the amino acid methionine), or for stopping it. To make a protein, an RNA intermediary called a messenger RNA (mRNA) is first made from the DNA by a protein called a polymerase. In the mRNA, the thymine bases are replaced by uracil (U). The mRNA then moves from the nucleus to the cytoplasm, where it locks onto a piece of protein-RNA machinery called a ribosome. The ribosome moves along the RNA molecule, reading the code. It interacts with molecules of transfer RNA, each of which is bound to a specific amino acid, and strings the amino acids together to form a protein.

5. Gene variants are called:
    a. Codons
    b. Alleles
    c. Methionine
    d. Phosphoribose

6. Which of the following protein sequences is encoded by the DNA base sequence GTTACAAAAAGA?
    a. Valine-threonine-lysine-arginine
    b. Valine-leucine-glycine-histidine
    c. Valine-aspartate-proline-serine
    d. Valine-serine-tyrosine-STOP

7. A polymerase begins reading the following DNA sequences with the first base shown. Which sequence specifies the end of a protein chain?
    a. GTACCCCTA
    b. GTACCCACA
    c. GTTAAAAGA
    d. GTTTAAGAC

8. The portion of a DNA molecule that encodes a single amino acid is a(n):
    a. Codon
    b. Allele
    c. Methionine
    d. Phosphoribose

9. Proteins are made by:
   a. Polymerases
   b. Transfer RNAs
   c. Ribosomes
   d. DNA molecules

10. Which of the following is NOT part of a gene?
    a. Guanine
    b. Codon
    c. Cytosine
    d. Ribosome

11. During the process of oogenesis, primary oocytes produce:
    a. Sperm
    b. Eggs
    c. Oogonia
    d. Stem cells

Questions 12-14 are based upon the following figure and text:
Electrochemical Battery

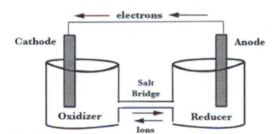

An electrochemical battery is a device powered by oxidation and reduction reactions that are physically separated so that the electrons must travel through a wire from the reducing agent to the oxidizing agent. The reducing agent loses electrons, and is oxidized in a reaction that takes place at an electrode called the anode. The electrons flow through a wire to the other electrode, the cathode, where an oxidizing agent gains electrons and is thus reduced. To maintain a net zero charge in each compartment, there is a limited flow of ions through a salt bridge. In a car battery, for example, the reducing agent is oxidized by the following reaction, which involves a lead (Pb) anode and sulfuric acid (H_2SO_4). Lead sulfate ($PbSO_4$), protons (H^+), and electrons (e^-) are produced:

$$Pb + H_2SO_4 \Rightarrow PbSO_4 + 2\ H^+ + 2\ e^-$$

At the cathode, which is made of lead oxide (PbO_2), the following reaction occurs. During this reaction, the electrons produced at the anode are used:

$$PbO_2 + H_2SO_4 + 2\ e^- + 2\ H^+ \Rightarrow PbSO_4 + 2\ H_2O$$

12. Electrons are produced by a chemical reaction that takes place at the:
    a. Anode
    b. Cathode
    c. Lead oxide electrode
    d. Oxidizer

13. In an oxidation reaction:
    a. An oxidizing agent gains electrons.
    b. An oxidizing agent loses electrons.
    c. A reducing agent gains electrons.
    d. A reducing agent loses electrons.

14. In a car battery, a product of the oxidation reaction that occurs at the cathode is:
    a. Lead oxide
    b. Lead
    c. Electrons
    d. Water

Questions 15-16 are based upon the following figure:

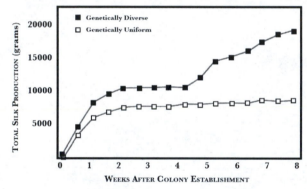

15. Colonies of silkworms containing the same number of genetically identical or genetically varying animals were established. For several weeks after the colonies were created, silk production was estimated by removing small samples of silk from the colonies and weighing them. The results are shown in the graph. The open symbols refer to the production of silk by genetically uniform worms, while the closed symbols refer to production of silk by genetically diverse worms. Which of the following conclusions can be drawn from the data?
    a. Genetically diverse worms produce more silk than genetically uniform worms.
    b. Genetically uniform worms produce more silk than genetically diverse worms.
    c. Genetically diverse silkworm colonies produce more silk than genetically uniform colonies.
    d. Genetically uniform silkworm colonies produce more silk than genetically diverse colonies.

16. If the generation time of a silkworm is about four weeks, which of the following hypotheses offers the best explanation for the difference in silk productivity between the two colonies?
    a. Genetically diverse silkworms produce silk longer than genetically uniform worms.
    b. Genetically diverse silkworms reproduce more than genetically uniform worms.
    c. Genetically diverse silkworms produce heavier silk than genetically uniform worms.
    d. Genetically uniform silkworms stop producing silk when they reproduce.

17. The digestion of starch begins:
    a. In the mouth
    b. In the stomach
    c. In the pylorus
    d. In the duodenum

Questions 18-22 are based upon the following figure and text:
Heat and the States of Matter

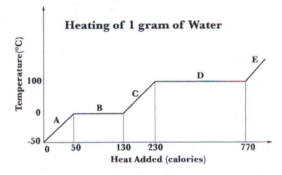

When the molecules of a substance absorb energy in the form of heat, they begin to move more rapidly. This increase in kinetic energy may be a more rapid vibration of molecules held in place in a solid, or it may be motion through molecular space in a liquid or a gas. Either way, it will be observed as either a change in temperature or a change in state. Heat has traditionally been measured in terms of calories. One calorie is equal to 4.186 Joules.

The specific heat capacity of a substance is the energy required to raise the temperature of 1 kg of the substance by 1°C. For water, this is 1000 calories. If heat continues to be applied to ice that is already at its melting point of 0°C, it remains at that temperature and melts into liquid water. The amount of energy required to produce this change in state is called the heat of fusion, and for water it is equal to 80 calories per gram. Similarly, the amount of energy required to change a gram of liquid water at 100°C into steam is called the heat of vaporization, and equals 540 calories.

The graph shows an experiment in calorimetry: 1 gram of water at -50°C is heated slowly from a solid state until it has all turned to gas. The temperature is monitored and reported as a function of the heat added to the system.

18. Heat is a form of:
    a. Potential energy
    b. Chemical energy
    c. Kinetic energy
    d. Temperature

19. Which of the following statements is true?
    a. Adding heat to a system always increases its temperature.
    b. The average speed of a gas molecule is slower than the average speed of a liquid molecule of the same substance.
    c. Adding heat to a system always increases the average speed of the molecules of which it is comprised.
    d. Heat must be added to liquid water to make ice.

20. In the diagram, in which region(s) of the diagram is liquid water present?
    a. B only
    b. B and C
    c. C only
    d. B, C, and D

21. How much heat must be added to 1 gram of water at 1°C to raise its temperature to 101°C?
    a. 100 calories
    b. 540 calories
    c. 770 calories
    d. 640 calories

22. In the diagram, as heat is added to the system, the water in region B can be said to be:
    a. Condensing
    b. Melting
    c. Freezing
    d. Evaporating

Questions 23-25 are based upon the following figure and text:
Neurons

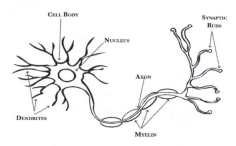

Messages travel between the brain and other parts of the body in the form of electrical impulses. A specialized cell, the neuron, produces these impulses. Neurons make up the brain and the nervous system. They number more than 100 billion in the human body.

Neurons have their own characteristic cellular anatomy consisting of three main parts. A cell body, containing a nucleus, is the center of metabolism. Dendrites project from the cell body and receive messages from neighboring neurons. At the other end, messages are sent through the *axon*, a long fiber extending from the cell body to the dendrites of other neurons, or to *effectors*, such as muscles, that perform actions based on neuronal input. Axons are sheathed in a material called myelin that helps nerve signals travel faster and farther.

At the end of the axon, messages must cross a narrow gap, the *synapse*, to reach effectors or the next neuron. Electrical impulses cannot cross this gap. The transfer of information from cell to cell occurs as a result of the release of chemical *neurotransmitters* into the space between the axon and the dendrites. The electrical impulse triggers the release of neurotransmitters into the synapse from swellings called *synaptic buds* at the axon terminal. They cross the synapse and bind to special *receptor* molecules on the dendrites of the next cell. Each neurotransmitter can bind only to a specific matching receptor, which triggers an appropriate response to the signal. This may be another electrical impulse, carrying the message along further, the contraction of a muscle, or some other effect.

23. A neuron consists of three main parts. These are:
    a. Effector, cell body, axon
    b. Dendrites, axon, cell body
    c. Dendrites, axon, receptor
    d. Synapse, axon, cell body

24. Chromosomes are located within the:
   a. Cell body
   b. Dendrites
   c. Axon
   d. Synapse

25. Which of the following statements is true?
   a. Information in neurons flows in one direction, from dendrites to axon.
   b. Information in the nervous system is carried by both electrical and chemical means.
   c. Myelin assists in the transmission of electrical, but not chemical, information.
   d. All of the above statements are true.

26. Of the following, the blood vessel containing the least-oxygenated blood is:
   a. The aorta
   b. The vena cava
   c. The pulmonary artery
   d. The capillaries

Question 27 is based upon the following figure:

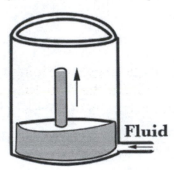

27. The figure shows an airtight cylinder into which fluid may be injected from the bottom. The cylinder contains a heavy piston which is raised by the injected fluid until the rod on top of the piston touches the top of the cylinder container. Fluids of different densities are injected, and an observer records the volume required to make the rod reach the top. Which of the following fluids will require the least injected volume?
   a. Water
   b. Oil
   c. Alcohol
   d. The same volume will be required for all fluids.

28. Mark and Nancy both measure the length of a pencil that is 15.1 cm. They use a ruler that has divisions for every mm along its length. Mark reports the length of the pencil as 15 cm. Nancy reports it as 15.0 cm. Which of the following statements is true?
    a. Mark's measurement is more precise.
    b. Nancy's measurement is more accurate.
    c. Mark's measurement is more accurate.
    d. Nancy's measurement is more precise.

29. All living organisms on Earth utilize:
    a. Oxygen
    b. Light
    c. Sexual reproduction
    d. A triplet genetic code

Questions 30-31 are based upon the following figure:

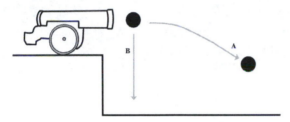

30. A cannon sits on top of a cliff 20 meters above an expanse of level ground. It fires a 5 kg cannonball horizontally (cannonball A) at 5 meters/second. At the same time, a second cannonball (cannonball B) is dropped from the same height. If air resistance is negligible, which cannonball will hit the ground first?
Note: The gravitational acceleration due to the Earth is 9.8 m/sec^2.
    a. Cannonball A
    b. Cannonball B
    c. Both will hit the ground at the same time.
    d. It will depend upon the temperature.

31. The cannon weighs 500 kg and is on wheels. It will recoil as a result of firing cannonball A. If friction is negligible, what will be the recoil speed of the cannon?
Note: Momentum is the product of mass and velocity.
    a. 5 meters/second
    b. 5000 cm/second
    c. 50 cm/second
    d. 5 cm/second

Questions 32-34 are based upon the following figure:

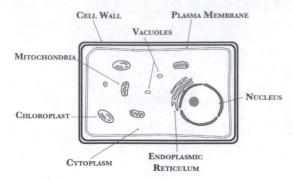

32. The cell depicted is a(n):
   a. Animal cell
   b. Plant cell
   c. Bacterial cell
   d. Virus

33. Which of the following structures contains DNA?
   a. Cytoplasm
   b. Vacuole
   c. Mitochondrion
   d. Nucleus

34. The mitochondria:
   a. Produce energy for the cell in the form of ATP.
   b. Are responsible for digesting starch.
   c. Are the sites of protein synthesis.
   d. Are not present in muscle cells.

35. If an organism is AaBb, which of the following combinations in the gametes is impossible?
   a. AB
   b. aa
   c. aB
   d. Ab

36. What is the typical result of mitosis in humans?
   a. two diploid cells
   b. two haploid cells
   c. four diploid cells
   d. four haploid cells

37. How does water affect the temperature of a living thing?
    a. Water increases temperature.
    b. Water keeps temperature stable.
    c. Water decreases temperature.
    d. Water does not affect temperature.

38. Which of the following substances allows for the fastest diffusion?
    a. gas
    b. solid
    c. liquid
    d. plasma

39. What is the oxidation number of hydrogen in CaH_2?
    a. +1
    b. −1
    c. 0
    d. +2

40. What is the name of the structure that prevents food from entering the airway?
    a. trachea
    b. esophagus
    c. diaphragm
    d. epiglottis

Social Studies

Questions 1-3 refer to the following chart:

Important Dates in the International Slave Trade

Date	Country	Event
1517	Spain	Begins regular slave trading
1592	Britain	Begins regular slave trading
1792	Denmark	Abolishes slave trade
1794	France	Abolishes slave trade
1807	Britain	Abolishes slave trade
1834	Britain	Abolishes slavery in all colonies
1865	United States	Abolishes slavery
1888	Brazil	Abolishes slavery

1. Which nation was the first to abolish slavery?
    a. Spain
    b. Britain
    c. Denmark
    d. France

2. If the United States had not won the Revolutionary War, when would slavery have been outlawed?
    a. 1792
    b. 1794
    c. 1807
    d. 1834

3. Which of the following conclusions is valid, based on your prior knowledge and the information on the chart?
    a. More slaves worked in Brazil than in any other nation.
    b. France realized its ideals of independence sooner than did the United States.
    c. Denmark was the largest slave-holding state in Europe.
    d. Britain freed enslaved peoples only after losing the Asian nations of the British Empire.

Questions 4-5 refer to the following map:

4. Which South American nations were the *last* to receive independence?
   a. Argentina and Paraguay
   b. Ecuador and Venezuela
   c. Bolivia and Uruguay
   d. Peru and Brazil

5. Which of the following generalizations is valid?
   a. The nations of North America were also fighting for independence at the same time as those nations in South America listed above.
   b. France lost most of its possessions in the New World as a result of these revolutions.
   c. Nations on the west coast received independence first.
   d. South America experienced multiple revolutions during the first three decades of the nineteenth century.

Questions 6-7 refer to the following chart:

Native Civilizations in Central and South America

Civilization	Location	Conquered by	Date Empires Ended
Maya	Central America	Internal collapse	950
Aztec	Mexico	Spanish under Hernán Cortés	1519
Inca	Peru	Spanish under Francisco Pizarro	1533

6. Mayan civilization is unlike the Aztec and Incan civilizations because
    a. it collapsed without an outside conqueror.
    b. it was the last empire to end.
    c. it was located in North America.
    d. it was conquered by the Spanish.

7. Which of the following conclusions is supported by the chart?
    a. Several nations in South America were conquered by Portugal.
    b. The Aztec civilization was the oldest of the three listed.
    c. Spain followed an aggressive policy of capturing new lands during the sixteenth century.
    d. Incan warriors tried to assist the Aztec against the Spanish.

Question 8 refers to the following passage:

> *In July 1862, President Abraham Lincoln told his cabinet that he intended to issue an emancipation proclamation before he did so. However, the Northern Army was not winning many battles of the Civil War that summer. Lincoln agreed with his cabinet advisers that it was a bad time to announce the intention. The following month, Horace Greeley, a prominent journalist, printed an open letter criticizing Lincoln for hesitating. The following is part of Lincoln's response.*
>
> *" ... My paramount object in this struggle is to save the Union, and it is not either to slave or destroy Slavery. If I could save the Union without freeing any slave, I would do it; and if I could save it by freeing all the slaves, I would do it; and if I could do it by freeing some and leaving others alone, I would also do that. What I do about Slavery and the colored race, I do because I believe it helps to save this Union; and what I forbear, I forbear because I do not believe it would help to save the Union. ... "*

8. Lincoln's stated primary objective is to
    a. free the slaves.
    b. repay slave owners for their losses.
    c. save the Union.
    d. win the war.

Questions 9-10 refer to the following chart:

Westward Migration

Year	Estimated Number of People Headed West
1844	2,000
1849	30,000
1854	10,000
1859	30,000
1864	20,000

9. Based on your general knowledge, what event caused the increased rate of westward movement between 1844 and 1848?
   a. Silver was discovered in Nevada.
   b. The Transcontinental Railroad was completed.
   c. Roman Catholics developed missions along the California coast.
   d. Gold was discovered at Sutter's Mill in California.

10. Given the increase of population, which of the following statements is most likely to be true?
   a. More children were being born in 1849 and 1858.
   b. Most of the new migrants were women who wanted to open businesses.
   c. The Civil War increased the westward migration.
   d. Cities and towns in the West grew and supported many businesses.

Questions 11-12 refer to the following chart:

Time Needed to Ship Freight from Cincinnati, Ohio, to New York City

Date	Route	Average Amount of Time
1817	Ohio River keelboat to Pittsburgh, wagon to Philadelphia, wagon or wagon and river to New York	52 days
1843–1851	Ohio River steamboat to Pittsburgh, canal to Philadelphia, railroad to New York	18–20 days
1852	Canal across Ohio, Lake Erie, Erie Canal, and Hudson River	18 days
1852	All rail via Erie Railroad and connecting lines	6–8 days
1850s	Steamboat to New Orleans and packet ship to New York	28 days

11. As a business owner in Cincinnati during the 1850s, which mode of transportation would you be most likely to choose?
   a. steamboat
   b. railroad
   c. canal
   d. keelboat

12. Which development in transportation resulted in the *most* time saved over its predecessor?
    a. railroad over steamboat and packet
    b. railroad over canals
    c. canal over steamboat and packet
    d. steamboat, canal, and railroad over keelboat and wagon

Questions 13-15 refer to the following chart:

Issues and Compromises in the United States Constitution

Issue	New Jersey Plan	Virginia Plan	Constitution
Legislative branch	A single house with members appointed by state legislatures	Two houses: Upper House with members elected by the people; Lower House elected by Upper House	Two houses: originally Senate members were elected by state legislatures, and representatives were and are still elected by the people.
Executive branch	Congress to choose an executive committee	Congress to choose a single president	President chosen by Electoral College, with electors selected by each of the states.
Judicial branch	Executive committee to appoint national judges	Congress chooses national judges	President appoints and Senate confirms Supreme Court judges.
Representation	Each state receives equal number of representatives	Representation to be based on wealth or population	Two houses created: House of Representatives based on population; Senate has two delegates from each state.

13. Which of the following conclusions can you draw on the issue of representation?
    a. Virginia's people were very poor.
    b. New Jersey originated the expression "Liberty, Equality, and Fraternity."
    c. Virginia was probably a state with many people.
    d. Many wealthy citizens lived in New Jersey.

14. The Virginia Plan for the legislative branch closely resembles that of
    a. the Mayflower Compact.
    b. Britain's Parliament.
    c. the government of the Sioux.
    d. France's monarchial system.

15. The Electoral College was created to resolve the issue of
    a. how the wealthiest people would be represented.
    b. who would appoint the Supreme Court members.
    c. how to elect senators.
    d. who would elect the chief executive.

Question 16 refers to the following passage:
    ARTICLE XXVII (Ratified July 1, 1971)
        Section 1. The right of citizens of the United States, who are
    eighteen years of age or older, to vote shall not be denied or abridged by
    the United States or by any State on account of age.

16. This amendment to the Constitution was ratified in part because of what historical reality?
    a. Women gained the right to vote.
    b. Suffrage was extended to all African Americans.
    c. Young men were being drafted to serve in the Vietnam War.
    d. The number of people under 21 years of age increased.

17. How did Egypt's geographical features most contribute to the stability of ancient Egyptian culture?
    a. The Nile River regularly and predictably flooded, irrigating crops.
    b. The expanse of the Nile River prevented Egyptians from settling elsewhere.
    c. The Valley of the Kings divided Upper Egypt from Lower Egypt.
    d. The Mediterranean Sea enabled contact between Egyptians and other ancient peoples.

18. How did Charlemagne's coronation as Holy Roman Emperor influence European politics?
    a. It united much of Western Europe under a single ruler.
    b. It strengthened papal authority regarding the right of political leaders to rule.
    c. It made Catholicism the official religion throughout Charlemagne's empire.
    d. It led to Charlemagne's renunciation of conquest by force.

19. During the 15th century, Johann Gutenberg invented a printing press with moveable type. How did his invention influence science?

    a. It did not influence science; the printing of Gutenberg Bibles directed public attention away from science and toward reforming the Catholic Church.

    b. It led to scientific advances throughout Europe by spreading scientific knowledge.

    c. It influenced scientific advancement in Germany only, where Gutenberg's press was based.

    d. It did not influence science; though texts with scientific knowledge were printed, distribution of these texts was limited.

20. Which statement best describes how Martin Luther's religious Reformation influenced Western civilization?

    a. It contributed to the decline of women's and girls' education.

    b. It weakened civil authorities in European towns.

    c. It contributed to the rise of individualism.

    d. It delayed reform within the Catholic Church itself.

21. How did World War II influence American society?

    a. Consumption decreased in postwar American society.

    b. Thousands of people moved to find work in war-related factories.

    c. Racially integrated army units helped desegregate American society.

    d. Japanese-Americans were banned from serving in the U.S. military.

22. How did the Truman Doctrine shape U.S. foreign policy after World War II?

    a. It influenced President Truman's decision to create commissions on civil rights.

    b. It shaped the U.S. role in rebuilding the economies of postwar Europe.

    c. It led the U.S. government to refrain from interfering with the U.S. economy.

    d. It led to U.S. military involvement in countries such as Korea.

23. The United States fought North Vietnam in the 1960s and 1970s primarily to:

    a. spread democracy modeled on the U.S. system.

    b. demonstrate U.S. power to the Soviet Union.

    c. protect U.S. trade interests in Southeast Asia.

    d. prevent the spread of communism.

24. Which statement best describes the significance of the Mayflower Compact on colonial America?

    a. It declared that the colonists were independent from King James.

    b. It served as a blueprint for the later Bill of Rights.

    c. It provided the Pilgrims the first written basis for laws in the New World.

    d. It established Puritanism as the official religion for Puritan colonies.

25. The link between female activists and the temperance movement in the 19th century is best explained by concerns regarding the relationship between alcohol and:
    a. racial violence.
    b. lost productivity.
    c. domestic violence.
    d. infertility.

26. How does the executive branch of a parliamentary democracy differ from that in the United States' form of government?
    a. It appoints the legislative branch.
    b. It is a committee of the judicial branch.
    c. It is appointed by the judicial branch.
    d. It is a committee of the legislative branch.

27. Which combination of factors is most likely to cause inflation?
    a. High unemployment and reduced production
    b. Credit restrictions and reduced production
    c. An oversupply of currency and a relatively low number of available goods
    d. An undersupply of currency and a relatively low number of available goods

28. How did Eli Whitney's invention of the cotton gin in 1793 most influence the U.S. economy?
    a. It elevated cotton as a basis of the Southern economy.
    b. It led to many smaller cotton plantations.
    c. It reduced the U.S. need to import cotton.
    d. It decreased the dependence of plantations on slave labor.

29. Arabic mathematics most contributed to the development of mathematics in the Western world by:
    a. founding the mathematics of calculus.
    b. using negative numbers in mathematical equations.
    c. founding the mathematics of probability.
    d. making important advances in algebra.

30. Which is the best description of how Jonas Salk's 1955 development of the polio vaccine most affected American society?
    a. The invention drastically reduced the incidence of polio in the United States.
    b. The vaccine caused polio in some people who received the vaccine.
    c. The announcement of the vaccine sparked a debate regarding the media and science.
    d. The vaccine ignited a vigorous search for a cancer vaccine.

31. Which of the following is true regarding the Treaty of Tordesillas?
	a. It was executed during the 1500s.
	b. It set up a "Line of Demarcation."
	c. It moved a line of demarcation east.
	d. It was between Spain and Portugal.

32. Which of the following conquistadores unwittingly gave smallpox to the Indians and destroyed the Aztec empire in Mexico?
	a. Balboa
	b. Ponce de Leon
	c. Cortes
	d. De Vaca

33. Which conquistador discovered the Mississippi River?
	a. Coronado
	b. De Soto
	c. Cortes
	d. De Leon

34. Which of the following statements is true regarding New Spain in the 1500s?
	a. New Spain had not yet developed any kind of class system.
	b. The Spanish originally imported Africans to use as slaves for labor.
	c. The hacienda system eventually gave way to the encomienda system.
	d. Conquistadores experienced shortages of labor in the New World.

35. Which of the following explorers was not involved in the search for a Northwest Passage?
	a. Verrazzano
	b. John Cabot
	c. Jacques Cartier
	d. All of the above explorers were involved in the search for a Northwest Passage.

36. Which of the following wars included no major army battles on American soil and no major changes in territories?
	a. Queen Anne's War
	b. King William's War
	c. King George's War
	d. The French and Indian War

37. Of the following, who was not a candidate for President of the USA in the 1824 election?
    a. Henry Clay
    b. William H. Crawford
    c. John Quincy Adams
    d. John C. Calhoun

38. Of the following areas that experienced innovations as a result of organized social reform in the 19th century, which one met with the most difficulty in its early years?
    a. Higher education
    b. Free public schools
    c. Mental institutions
    d. Prison reforms

39. Which of the following was not instrumental in enabling Republicans to take control of the House and the Senate in the 1994 Congressional elections during the Clinton administration?
    a. Alleged impropriety in the "Whitewater" deal
    b. Rumors alleging sexual misconduct by Clinton
    c. Debates on healthcare and gays in the military
    d. All of the above were factors that helped the Republicans gain control of Congress.

40. Of the following, which statement about the US economy in the 1990s is correct?
    a. By the year 2000, the US economy was increasing at a rate of 5% a year.
    b. The rate of unemployment in America at this time dropped to 6%.
    c. The rates of productivity and of inflation in the US were about the same.
    d. The US stock market's total value had doubled in only six years.

Answers and Explanations

English

1. C: The clock is ebony, symbolizing death, and it is placed against the western wall of the room. The sun sets in the west, another symbol of death. Words such as *dull, heavy,* and *monotonous* also provide a clue. The momentary pause of the orchestra members at the end of each hour prefigures the final pause that all the dancers and orchestra members will make. Poe writes that "the giddiest grew pale," an allusion to the pallor of death. Other words suggesting the finality of death are *nervousness, disconcert, tremulousness,* and *meditation.*

2. D: The passage refers to musicians, but choice A is not accurate because the passage also mentions waltzers who had to stop dancing when the musicians of the orchestra stopped playing. There is no indication of food in the descriptions given of the apartment where the clock is located. A garden party would be held outdoors while this is clearly an interior scene. This need for an outdoor setting is true as well of a boating party. Thus the first three options are all incorrect, leaving only choice D.

3. B: Because of the sound of the chiming clock, the musicians stop, which means the dancers stop as well. Choice A is not accurate. The passage makes no mention of food or a meal or even of the host. Although an uninvited guest makes an appearance in the story, that scene is not included here, so choice C is incorrect. The passage does not indicate that the dancers are masked nor that they are asked to remove their masks. This means option D is not correct.

4. D: The passage refers specifically to "the Time that flies," a reminder of the brevity of life. The pause of both orchestra and dancers when the clock strikes is simply a prelude to the final pause. There is not enough information in the passage to indicate that a king even exists, nor is there mention of the skill of the orchestra. Thus A can be eliminated. There is no indication of the need for police, making option B incorrect. The clock seems to be in good working order, and thus C is incorrect.

5. C: *mysterious* and *forbidding.* The passage does not answer the mystery of why the orchestra and dancers regularly halt at the sound of the chimes. Many of the words—such as *ebony, disconcert, pale, confused,* and *tremulousness*—in the passage refer to puzzles or gloominess. The other choices are extremes that cannot be supported. Choices A and B are too light for the passage, whereas choices 4 is too negative. The passage hints at negative events to come, but these are not expressed in the passage itself.

6. A: Dickinson's words *oppresses, hurt, despair,* and *imperial affliction* confirm that depression is the best answer. The poem certainly does not contain any words that could refer to joy, making choice B incorrect. Likewise, The third option, uncertainty, cannot be supported by the text. There is no sense of surprise in the lines; rather, the certain slant of light can almost be predicted as coming on winter afternoons. Thus choice D can be eliminated. Dickinson is also not excited by but resigned to this melancholy.

7. C: A simile is a comparison of two unlike things using the words *like* or *as*. Dickinson says the slant of light oppresses like "the weight of cathedral tunes." Personification is the attributing of human qualities to something not human, a device not used here, so choice B is incorrect. A metaphor is a direct comparison, which is not the case in these lines, making choice D wrong. Onomatopoeia refers to the use of words that suggest what they are, such as *bang*.

8. B: Personification is the attributing of human qualities to something not human. Here, the landscape listens and shadows hold their breath, mimicking human or animal behavior. Assonance is the repetition of vowel sounds, which is not evident here, making option A wrong. A simile is a comparison of two unlike things using the words *like* or *as*. Because that is not the case here, choice C is incorrect. A metaphor is a direct comparison, which is not the case in these lines, making choice D wrong. Onomatopoeia refers to the use of words that suggest what they are, such as *bang*.

9. D: because the first stanza clearly refers to "winter afternoons." Solstice is not a season but a day on which seasons change, making the second response incorrect. The second response, summer, is not supported in the text of the poem. Likewise, Choice C, autumn, is absent from the text. The reference to the "look of death" in the final line of the poem cannot be construed as anything except winter. The idea that the poem refers to the season of spring, new beginnings, cannot be supported from the text.

10. D: The question asks for the word that does not fit with the mood of the poetry. The mood of the poem evokes a sort of quiet despair to which stanza three alludes. A cathedral is not part of the idea of despair but often signifies faith and hope. Choice A is incorrect; *hurt* is in alignment with the feeling of the poem. Likewise, *scar* is a word that fits with the mood, so choice B can be eliminated. *Despair* is used in the poem itself and complements the mood. Choice C, therefore, is incorrect.

11. A: Volleyball is a team sport that follows the verb "to play," whereas individual sports like yoga follow the verb "to do."

12. B: The term "student" is general, so the relative clause is essential to the meaning of the sentence and should not be separated out by commas.

13. B: The second sentence is the clearest, since there are misplaced modifiers and verb confusion in the other sentences.

14. D: The word "every" is a singular noun and should be followed by a singular pronoun. In this case, the only singular pronoun is "her."

15. A: The phrasal verb "to put up with" means to have to deal with something or someone.

16. D: The future tense is will + the infinitive, in this case "will study."

17. B: This should be an adverb, and the correct spelling is "sympathetically."

18. A: The subject of this sentence, "a team," is singular, so the verb also should be singular.

19. B: This sentence is in the past tense so the phrasal verb should also be in the past tense.

20. A: The correct spelling is "believes."

21. B: The correct spelling is "presents."

22. D: The correct spelling is "authority."

23. A: The correct spelling is "traveled."

24. C: The word "precipitous" means "steep."

25. B: The word "obscure" means "unclear" and "difficult to understand."

26. C: The word "remiss" means "negligent or forgetful."

27. D: The passage indicates that the formula increases or boosts the absorption of minerals in the body.

28. B: The directions say to mix equal parts of all the herbs listed.

29. D: The dosage indicates not to exceed four tablespoons in a 24-hour period, so the patient should take it no more than every six hours.

30. C: All methods are used in the cooking process except for whisking.

31. C: The professor argues that after a fire, small, woody material is left on the tops of trees where a fire cannot reach. Therefore, the material is unavailable as fuel for future fires.

32. B: Since the plot that was salvage logged (Plot A) burned with greater severity than the unmanaged plot (Plot B), the study supports the professor's view that salvage logging increases the risk and severity of fire.

33. A: The forest manager feels that by removing dead or dying material through salvage logging, less fuel is available for future fires.

34. D: The professor states the opposite of answer choice D and says that larger trees found in old growth forests are more resistant to fire than small, younger trees.

35. C: A study looking at the regeneration of seedlings in both logged and unmanaged forests would help to clarify and/or validate both arguments, since both the manager and the professor discuss the importance of seedling growth following a fire.

36. C: The passage states that he was given this title since he was the first to explain how organisms change over time.

37. A: The tone and purpose of this passage is to inform the reader.

38. D: The passage explains that finches with longer, sharper beaks were able to reach insects more easily than finches with shorter beaks, giving them an advantage over the other finches on the island.

39. B: The island finches were different from the mainland finches, so their geographical separation over time increased the diversity of finches

40. D: The passage states that the island finches differed from the mainland finches by the shape of their beaks and in their diet.

Mathematics

1. C: The total amount of the bill is: $3.70/x = 8/100$; $370 = 8x$; $x = \$46.25$.

2. D: First set the relationship up and solve for the number of packs: $x/2=5/\text{packs}$; $x(\text{packs}) = 10$; packs $= 10/x$.

3. A: The correct expression is: $J = K/2 + 5$.

4. A: Plugging in x and y, you get $(4(3) - 4) + (-10 + 4)$, which is $8 + (-6)$, or $8 - 6 = 2$.

5. B: The average rate of cooling is: $(86° - 38°) / 9$ hrs; $48° / 9 = 5.33°$ F per hour.

6. D: Calculate the weighted average of the 3 tests: $(80 + 75 + 92)/3 = 82.33$; Calculate the average of the 2 oral quizzes: $(22 + 19)/2 = 20.5$; $(20.5/25) \times 100 =82$. Multiply each grade by its weight, and then add them all up to determine the final grade: $(82.33 \times 0.45) + (88 \times 0.25) + (91 \times 0.15) + (82 \times 0.15) = 85$.

7. B: Double the number that is added to the previous number. So, 4+2=6, 6+4=10, 10+8=18, 18+16=34, and 34+32=66.

8. A: 1 kilometer is equal to 100,000 centimeters. 250 cm / 100,000 cm/km= 0.0025 km.

9. B: First convert to feet: $144/12 = 12$ feet; $168/12 = 14$ feet. $12 \times 1.4 = 16.8$ feet; $14 \times 1.4 = 19.6$ feet.

10. A: $(x^2)^3 = x^{(2 \times 3)} = x^6$; $(y^2)^5 = y^{(2 \times 5)} = y^{10}$; $(y^4)^3 = y^{(4 \times 3)} = y^{12}$; $y^{10} \cdot y^{12} = y^{(10+12)} = y^{22}$.

11. B: $(x^2)^5 y^6 z^2 / x^4 (y^3)^4 z^2$; $x^{(2x5) - 4} = x^6$; $y^{6 - (3x4)} = y^{-6}$; $z^{2 - 2} = z^0$ or 1; so the answer is $x^6 y^{-6}$.

12. A: Using the Pythagorean theorem: $25^2 + 35^2 = c^2$. $625 + 1225 = c^2$. $c = \sqrt{1850} = 43.01$.

13. A: $V = \pi r^2 h$. $V = 3.14 \times (3^2) \times 12$. $3.14 \times 9 \times 12 = 339.12$.

14. B: The equation for perimeter (P) = 2L + 2W. So, $600 = 2(250) + 2W$. Solve for W: $600 - 500 = 2W$. $100 = 2W$. $W = 50$.

15. C: He would have to pull out at least 9 (5 + 2 + 1 + 1) to make sure he has a yellow one.

16. B: The easiest pair to test is the third: $y = 4$ and $x = 0$. Substitute these values in each of the given equations and evaluate. Choice B gives $4 = 0 + 4$, which is a true statement. None of the other answer choices is correct for this number set.

17. D: At the point of intersection, the y-coordinates are equal on both lines so that $2x + 3 = x - 5$. Solving for x, we have $x = -8$. Then, evaluating y with either equation yields $y = 2(-8) + 3 = -16 + 3 = -13$ or $y = -8 - 5 = -13$

18. A: Evaluate as follows: $2f(x) - 3 = 2(2x^2 + 7) - 3 = 4x^2 + 14 - 3 = 4x^2 + 11$.

19. D: The stock first increased by 10%, that is, by $10 (10% of $100) to $110 per share. Then, the price decreased by $11 (10% of $110) so that the sale price was $110-$11 = $99 per share, and the sale price for 50 shares was 99 x $50 = $4950.

20. D: The sides of a triangle must all be greater than zero. The sum of the lengths of the two shorter sides must be greater than the length of the third side. Since we are looking for the minimum value of the perimeter, assume the longer of the two given sides, which is 6, is the longest side of the triangle. Then the third side must be greater than 6 – 4 = 2. Since we are told the sides are all integer values, the last side must be 3 units in length. Thus, the minimum length for the perimeter is 4+6+3 = 13 units.

21. C: The hypotenuse must be the longest side of a right triangle, so it must be the lengths of the other two sides that are given as 6 and 8 units. Calculate the length of the hypotenuse, H, from the Pythagorean Theorem:
$H^2 = S_1^2 + S_2^2 = 6^2 + 8^2 = 36 + 64 = 100$, which yields $H = 10$ and the perimeter equals 10+6+8 = 24.

22. A: The area of a triangle equals half the product of base times height. Since the base passes through the center, we have base = 2 r and height = r, so that the area A is $A = \dfrac{r \times 2r}{2} = r^2$

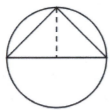

23. D: The probability of getting three aces in a row is the product of the probabilities for each draw. For the first ace, that is 4 in 52, since there are 4 aces in a deck of 52 cards. For the second, it is 3 in 51, since 3 aces and 51 cards remain; and for the third, it is 2 in 50. So the overall probability, P, is
$P = \frac{4}{52} \times \frac{3}{51} \times \frac{2}{50} = \frac{24}{132600} = \frac{1}{5525}$.

24. C: This can be solved as two equations with two unknowns. Since the integers are consecutive with $p > n$, we have $p - n = 1$, so that $p = 1 + n$. Substituting this value into $p + n = 15$ gives $1 + 2n = 15$, or $n = \dfrac{14}{2} = 7$.

25. B: The square is one whose diagonal corresponds to the diameter of the circle. This allows calculation of the side a by the Pythagorean Theorem, where the diameter is $d = 2r$: $d^2 = 4r^2 = a^2 + a^2$. Thus, $4r^2 = 2a^2$, and the area of the square $a^2 = 2r^2$.

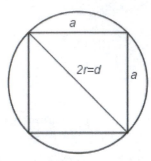

26. D: Remember that when you multiply like bases, you add the exponents, and when you divide like bases, you subtract the exponents.
$$(xy)^{7y} - (xy)^y = (xy)^y \left[(xy)^{7y-y} - 1 \right] = (xy)^y \left[(xy)^{6y} - 1 \right]$$

27. B: If the averages are equal, then we have $\dfrac{x + y + z}{3} = \dfrac{a + b + c}{3}$, so that it must be true that $(x + y + z) = (a + b + c)$. Therefore the average of all six numbers is
$$\dfrac{(x + y + z) + (a + b + c)}{6} = \dfrac{2(x + y + z)}{6} = \dfrac{x + y + z}{3} = 23.$$

28. C: The line in the graph has a negative slope and a positive y-axis intercept, so the factor multiplying the variable x, or the slope, must be negative, and the constant, or y-intercept, must be positive.

29. B: as the volume of a rectangular box can be determined using the formula $V = l * w * h$. This means that the volume of a rectangular box can be determined by multiplying the length of the base of the box by the width of the box and multiplying that product by the height of the box. Therefore, the volume of the box described in this question is equal to 5 * 7 * 9, or 315 in³. (A) is incorrect because it provides the volume of a cylinder with a diameter of 9 inches and a height of 7 inches. (C) is incorrect because it provides the area of a rectangle with a base of 5 inches and a width of 9 inches. (D) is incorrect because it states the area of a rectangle with a base of 5 inches and a width of 7 inches.

30. D: The circular area covered by the sprinkler is πr^2, so the difference is obtained as $\pi \times 8^2 - \pi \times 6^2 = \pi(64 - 36) = 28\pi = 87.92$.

31. D: which is obtained by moving the second term to the right of the equality and changing its sign.

32. B: The radius, R, of the satellite's orbit is the sum of the Earth's radius plus the satellite's orbital altitude, or $R = 4400$ miles. The circumference of the circular orbit is therefore $C = 2\pi r = 2\pi(4400) = 8800\pi$ miles. Since 40 minutes is one third of the satellite's 120-minute orbital time, it traverses one third of this distance in that time. So the distance, $D = \dfrac{40}{120} \times 2\pi \times 4400 = 9210.66$ miles, using 3.14 for π.

33. D: The line in the graph has a constant value of y, one that does not change regardless of the value of x. This is a special case of the equation for the straight line, $y = mx + b$, for which $m = 0$.

34. D: When no tickets are sold, $N = 0$, and $0 = 25000 - 0.1p^2$, so that $0.1p^2 = 25000$, and $p^2 = \dfrac{25000}{0.1} = 250{,}000 = 2500 \times 100 = 50^2 \times 10^2$, so that $p = 50 \times 10 = 500$.

35. B: Profit equals (tickets sold) x (price) – cost. The number of tickets sold is given by the equation in Question 34. Multiplying this expression by price, p, gives $25{,}000p - 0.1p^3$, and subtracting cost gives the expression in Choice B.

36. A: The median of a set of numbers is one for which the set contains an equal number of greater and lesser values. Besides Z, there are 8 numbers in the set, so that 4 must be greater and 4 lesser than Z. The 4 smallest values are 5, 7, 9, and 12. The 4 largest are 16, 18, 23, and 44. So Z must fall between 12 and 16.

37. C: If Q is divisible by both 7 and 2, it must be a multiple of 14, which is the least common multiple of both 2 and 7. Therefore, if one adds another multiple of 14 to Q, it will also be divisible by both 2 and 7. Of the choices given, only 28 is a multiple of 14.

38. C: $6\sqrt{10} = \sqrt{36}\sqrt{10} = \sqrt{360}$

39. A: This is a right triangle, since the two angles shown add up to 90 degrees, and the remaining angle must therefore be 90 degrees. For a right triangle, the length of a side is related to the hypotenuse by the sine of the opposite angle. Thus $A = C\sin(30^o)$ and since the sine of a 30-degree angle is 0.5, $A = C/2$.

40. A: Since the second line, $y = 3$, is a vertical, the intersection must occur at a point where $y = 3$. If $x = -1.5$, the equation describing the line is satisfied: $(2 \times [-1.5] + 3) = 0$

Science

1. C: A normal sperm must contain one of each of the human chromosome pairs. There are 23 chromosome pairs in all. Twenty-two of these are *autosomal* chromosomes, which do not play a role in determining gender. The remaining pair consists of either two X chromosomes in the case of a female, or of an X and a Y chromosome in the case of a male. Therefore, a normal sperm cell will contain 22 autosomal chromosomes and either an X or a Y chromosome, but not both.

2. B: The pitch of a sound depends upon the frequency of the sound wave. The higher the frequency, the higher the sound's pitch. Frequency varies inversely with wavelength, so that a higher pitched sound with a higher frequency will have a longer wavelength. The volume of a sound depends upon the degree to which the molecules of air (or any other medium through which the sound travels) are compressed. This compression is represented by the wave amplitude. The greater the amplitude, the louder the sound.

3. D: The waves corresponding to the two emitted sounds will be added, and what will be heard by the observer will be the sum of the two waves. Since these waves are one-half of a wavelength apart, they are perfectly out of phase, and they will cancel one another out. That is, the amplitude peak of one wave will coincide in space with the amplitude trough of the other. This phenomenon is called cancellation. The opposite is also possible: if the waves were perfectly in phase, they would combine additively, producing a much louder sound. Finally, if the waves were out of phase with one another, this would cause the intensity of the sound to vary.

4. A: Evolutionary fitness is a measure of the ability to transmit genes to subsequent generations. As such, it is characterized by the ability to produce offspring. Although the male wolf described in choice A died young, he lived long enough to produce 4 offspring, more than any of the animals described in the other choices. Therefore, his genes have the greatest chance of being passed on. It is important to realize that evolutionary "success," or fitness, simply requires an organism to live long enough to reproduce, and is measured exclusively by reproductive success.

5. B: An allele is a variant of the original DNA sequence for a gene. It may differ from the original by a single base (for example, it may contain a C in place of a G), or by a whole region in which the sequence of bases differ. It may have extra bases in it (insertions) or be missing some material (deletions). Whatever the difference, it will result in RNA, and subsequently a protein, whose sequence differs from that of the original. Sometimes, these differing proteins are defective. They may result in disease or developmental anomalies. Sometimes they are benign, as in the difference between blue and brown eyes in humans.

6. A: The sequence can be read directly from the table. It is read three bases at a time, since three bases constitute a codon and provide the information required to specify a single amino acid. In the sequence given, the first codon is GTT. The table shows that this corresponds to the amino acid valine. Similarly, the second codon is ACA, which corresponds to threonine. The third codon, AAA, corresponds to lysine, and the fourth, AGA, to arginine. Each sequence of amino acids produces a specific protein which is different from any other.

7. D: Begin parsing each sequence from the first base and break it into triplets to represent each codon. The sequence in choice A, for example, is GTA CCC CTA, representing valine-proline-leucine. Only the sequence in choice D contains one of the three STOP codons, which are TGA, TAA, and TAG. In choice D, the second codon is TAA. When the polymerase reaches this codon, it will begin the process of disengaging from the DNA, ending the mRNA copy and ultimately the protein product of the gene.

8. A: The DNA molecule is a long chain of phosphoribose to which bases are attached. The sequence of bases specifies the individual amino acids that are chained together to make a protein. There are 4 different bases and 23 different amino acids. Each amino acid is specified by a three-base "word," called a codon in the language of DNA. As the table shows, the 4 bases can be strung together in 64 different ways to encode the 23 different amino acids (plus STOP signals), so that some amino acids may be specified by more than a single codon.

9. C: While proteins are *encoded* in the DNA, they are actually *produced* by ribosomes, which string the proteins together from amino acids in the cell's cytoplasm. The information required to string proteins into the correct sequence is provided by mRNAs that are made by polymerases, which read the codons in the DNA. Transfer RNAs bring the amino acids to the ribosomes, where they are assembled into proteins.

10. D: Phosphoribose provides the backbone of the DNA chain of which genes are comprised. There, bases such as cytosine and guanine are strung together and organized into triplets known as codons, which encode the protein to be made. The protein itself will be assembled far from the gene, which is in the cell's nucleus, by the ribosome, which is in the cytoplasm of the cell.

11. B: Oogenesis is the process that gives rise to the ovum, or egg, in mammals. The oocyte is the immature egg cell in the ovary. In humans, one oocyte matures during each menstrual cycle. It develops first into an intermediate form called the ootid, and eventually into an ovum. The prefix *oo-* is derived from Greek, and means "egg."

12. A: The reactions described in the text are ones during which negatively charged electrons are produced by a reaction that reduces the positively-charged lead anode. The reducing agent, in turn, is oxidized by this reaction. These electrons travel

through the wire to the negatively-charged cathode, where they react with the sulfuric acid oxidizer and reduce it, forming lead sulfate. In a car battery, the anode is the positively-charged electrode, and is normally indicated by a red marking.

13. A: In an oxidation reaction, an oxidizing agent gains electrons from a reducing agent. By contributing electrons, the reducing agent reduces (makes more negative) the charge on the oxidizer. In the car battery, reduction of the positively-charged anode provides electrons, which then flow to the cathode, where an oxidation takes place. In an oxidation, an oxidizing agent increases (makes more positive) the charge on a reducer. In this way, the extra electrons in the negatively charged cathode are neutralized by the surrounding oxidizing agent.

14. D: The reaction described in the text is one during which two water molecules (H_2O) are produced for each lead oxide (PbO_2) molecule that reacts at the cathode.

15. C: The data indicates that up until about 4 weeks, the silk production from both colonies was similar. This suggests that the worms from each colony produced the same amount of silk, and that choices A and B are incorrect. The data does indicate that, over the long term, the silk produced by the entire colony of genetically diverse worms was greater than the silk produced by the entire colony of genetically uniform worms. This might be because the worms produce for a longer time, or because of some other mechanism. The experiment does not indicate what that mechanism might be.

16. B: The increase in productivity from the diverse culture occurs at about 4 weeks, coinciding with the time at which new worms are hatched and begin to produce silk.

17. A: The digestion of starch begins with its exposure to the enzyme amylase, which is present in the saliva. Amylase attacks the glycosidic bonds in starch, cleaving them to release sugars. This is the reason why some starchy foods may taste sweet if they are chewed extensively. Another form of amylase is produced by the pancreas, and continues the digestion of starches in the upper intestine. The di- and tri-saccharides, which are the initial products of this digestion, are eventually converted to glucose, a monosaccharide that is easily absorbed through the intestinal wall.

18. C: Because the addition of heat causes the molecules of a substance to increase their rate of motion, it is considered a form of kinetic energy. The temperature of a substance is proportional to the kinetic energy of the molecules of which it is made. Addition of heat to a system usually results in an increase in temperature, but temperature is not a form of heat. It is a measure of the amount of kinetic energy present in a system.

19. C: Energy in the form of heat is always absorbed by the molecules of a substance to make them move faster. During a change of state, some molecules are absorbing

energy and escaping the solid phase to become liquid, or escaping the liquid phase to become gas. Since molecules in a gas move faster than those in a liquid and molecules in a liquid move faster than those in a gas, the average speed increases. Note that choice E is incorrect since the heat of vaporization for water is greater than its heat of fusion.

20. D: In region B of the graph, the water is at 0°C. Heat is being added to it and it is progressively changing to a liquid. In region C, the temperature is climbing from 0°C to 100°C, and all of the water is in a liquid phase. In region D, the water is at 100°C, and is progressively changing to a gas as more energy is added. Once it has all changed to a gas, the temperature will once again increase as more heat is added (region E).

21. D: Water at 1°C is in the liquid phase. Using the definition of the specific heat capacity given in the text, it will take 99 calories to raise the temperature of 1 gm of liquid water to 100°C. Using the definition of the heat of vaporization given in the text, it will take an additional 540 calories to turn it into the gaseous phase once it reaches 100°C. Finally, an additional calorie must be added to bring the temperature of the gas up to 101°C. Therefore, the total amount of heat which must be added is 640 calories.

22. B: Region B of the graph represents the transition between the solid and liquid phases of water. If heat is added to the system, solid water melts into liquid. Conversely, if heat is removed from the system, liquid water will freeze in this region of the graph. Similarly, region D represents the transition between liquid and gaseous water. In this region, water either evaporates or condenses, depending upon whether heat is added to or removed from it. Sublimation (choice E) is the direct transition from the solid to the gaseous phase, which occurs only under conditions of very low pressure.

23. B: The cell body, containing the nucleus, is the control center of the cell and the site of its metabolic activity. Dendrites, which extend from this cell body, receive signals from other cells in the form of neurotransmitters. This triggers an electrical impulse, which travels down the axon to the next cell on the route of the signal. At the end of the axon, neurotransmitters are again released, cross the synapse, and act upon the following cell.

24. A: The cell body contains the nucleus, as shown in the diagram. In all *eukaryotic* cells (cells containing a nucleus), the nucleus is the site where the chromosomes reside. The chromosomes carry the genes, which direct the activities of the neuron.

25. D: Information flow is in one direction, moving from dendrite to axon within a neuron, and then crossing from axon to dendrite to move from cell to cell at the synapse. The electrical impulse that carries information along the axon is assisted by myelin, but there is no myelin at the synapse, so it can have no role there. The

flow of information across the synapse is achieved through the medium of neurotransmitters, which diffuse across the synapse to interact with dendritic receptors on the other side.

26. C: he pulmonary artery carries oxygen-depleted blood from the heart to the lungs, where CO_2 is released and the supply of oxygen is replenished. This blood then returns to the heart through the pulmonary artery, and is carried through the aorta and a series of branching arteries to the capillaries, where the bulk of gas exchange with the tissues occurs. Oxygen-depleted blood returns to the heart through branching veins (the femoral veins bring it from the legs) into the vena cava, which carries it again to the heart. Since the pulmonary artery is the last step before replenishment of the blood's oxygen content, it contains the blood which is the most oxygen depleted.

27. D: Since the cylinder is airtight, the piston cannot sink into the injected fluids, so it will not displace a volume of fluid equal to its weight. Since liquids are not compressible, the density of the injected fluid makes no difference in this experiment. Equal volumes of any fluid will raise the cylinder by an equal amount.

28. D: The terms *accuracy* and *precision*, often used interchangeably in informal speech, have specific meanings as scientific terms. Accuracy describes how close a measurement is to the actual dimension that is being measured. In this case, both measurements have the same accuracy. Precision is the degree of exactness that characterizes a measurement, or the number of significant figures with which it can be reported. Nancy's measurement is the more precise of the two, because she has reported the length to the nearest millimeter, whereas Mark's measurement is to the nearest centimeter. Note that the ruler cannot measure the length to a greater precision than that which Nancy has specified because the millimeter is its smallest division.

29. D: All living organisms on Earth utilize the same triplet genetic code, in which a three-nucleotide sequence called a codon provides information corresponding to a particular amino acid to be added to a protein. In contrast, many organisms, especially certain types of bacteria, do not use oxygen. These organisms live in oxygen-poor environments, and may produce energy through fermentation. Other organisms may live in dark environments, such as in caves or deep underground. Many organisms reproduce asexually by budding or self-fertilization, and only the most evolutionarily-advanced organisms make use of neurotransmitters in their nervous systems.

30. C: Both cannonballs will be subject to a vertical acceleration due to the force of gravity. Although there is an additional horizontal component to the velocity of cannonball A, its vertical velocity will be the same. In each case, the height of the object at time t seconds will be $h = -\frac{1}{2}t^2 + 20$.

31. D: First, note that 5 meters equals 500 cm, so the horizontal speed of the cannonball is 500 cm/sec. Momentum must be conserved in the recoiling system. The vertical motion due to gravity can be ignored, since it involves conservation of momentum between the cannonball and the Earth rather than the cannon. In the horizontal dimension, conservation of momentum dictates that $MV = mv$, where M and V represent the mass and the velocity of the cannon, and m and v represent the mass and the velocity of the cannonball. Solving for V gives

$$V = \frac{1}{M} \times mv = \frac{1}{500} \times 5 \times 500 = 5 \text{ cm/sec.}$$

32. B: This cell possesses both chloroplasts and a cell wall, which are characteristic of plant cells and are not found in the other cell types listed. Chloroplasts, which contain the pigment chlorophyll, are the engines of photosynthesis, and provide the cell with energy from sunlight. The cell wall, made of cellulose, provides a protective covering.

33. D: The nucleus houses the chromosomes, which are made of both DNA and a protein component. The chromosomes contain the genetic code in the form of the particular sequence of bases that make up the DNA chain.

34. A: Mitochondria provide chemical energy for the cell in the form of ATP, or adenosine triphosphate, which is used in a variety of cellular reactions. They do so by converting nutritional energy sources, such as glucose, through a complex series of chemical reactions that take place upon the extensive membrane system located within the mitochondria's outer membranes.

35. B: It is impossible for an *AaBb* organism to have the *aa* combination in the gametes. It is impossible for each letter to be used more than one time, so it would be impossible for the lowercase *a* to appear twice in the gametes. It would be possible, however, for *Aa* to appear in the gametes, since there is one uppercase *A* and one lowercase *a*. Gametes are the cells involved in sexual reproduction. They are germ cells.

36. A: The typical result of mitosis in humans is two diploid cells. *Mitosis* is the division of a body cell into two daughter cells. Each of the two produced cells has the same set of chromosomes as the parent. A diploid cell contains both sets of homologous chromosomes. A haploid cell contains only one set of chromosomes, which means that it only has a single set of genes.

37. B: Water stabilizes the temperature of living things. The ability of warm-blooded animals, including human beings, to maintain a constant internal temperature is known as *homeostasis*. Homeostasis depends on the presence of water in the body. Water tends to minimize changes in temperature because it takes a while to heat up or cool down. When the human body gets warm, the blood vessels dilate and blood

moves away from the torso and toward the extremities. When the body gets cold, blood concentrates in the torso. This is the reason why hands and feet tend to get especially cold in cold weather.

38. A: Diffusion is fastest through gases. The next fastest medium for diffusion is liquid, followed by plasma, and then solids. In chemistry, diffusion is defined as the movement of matter by the random motions of molecules. In a gas or a liquid, the molecules are in perpetual motion. For instance, in a quantity of seemingly immobile air, molecules of nitrogen and oxygen are constantly bouncing off each other. There is even some miniscule degree of diffusion in solids, which rises in proportion to the temperature of the substance.

39. B: The oxidation number of the hydrogen in CaH_2 is –1. The oxidation number is the positive or negative charge of a monoatomic ion. In other words, the oxidation number is the numerical charge on an ion. An ion is a charged version of an element. Oxidation number is often referred to as oxidation state. Oxidation number is sometimes used to describe the number of electrons that must be added or removed from an atom in order to convert the atom to its elemental form.

40. D: The epiglottis covers the trachea during swallowing, thus preventing food from entering the airway. The trachea, also known as the windpipe, is a cylindrical portion of the respiratory tract that joins the larynx with the lungs. The esophagus connects the throat and the stomach. When a person swallows, the esophagus contracts to force the food down into the stomach. Like other structures in the respiratory system, the esophagus secretes mucus for lubrication.

Social Studies

1. C: Denmark abolished slavery in 1792. Each of the remaining answers is incorrect. France did not abolish slavery for another two years, waiting until 1794. The chart does not include information on Spain's abolishing of slavery. Britain was the third European nation to abolish slavery, in 1807. The United States did not abolish slavery until 1865, following the Civil War. The last nation on the chart, Brazil, postponed abolition until 1888. The other, earliest dates on the chart, 1517 and 1592, refer to the beginnings of European nations' involvement in the slave trade.

2. D: The United States was a British colony before winning independence and so would have been required to end slavery in 1834, when slavery was abolished in all British colonies. Each of the other options is incorrect. Denmark abolished slavery in 1792, but the colonies did not have a major relationship with that nation. In 1794, France forbad slavery, but most of the colonies were not French possessions by the time of the American Revolution, France having ceded land to Britain following the French and Indian War in 1763. In 1807, Britain ended slavery but did not yet extend that rule to its colonies. The final date, 1888, refers to the end of slavery in Brazil.

3. B: France's Revolution began in 1789. Only five years later, the slave trade was abolished, which seems to indicate an extension and realization of the ideals of independence. The United States Revolution began in 1776; almost a century passed before slavery finally ended, in 1865. None of the other conclusions can be supported from the chart. Brazil was a large slave-holding nation, but that information is not included. It is unlikely that Denmark, a small nation with few colonies, would have been a large slave-holding state. The Asian nations remained in Britain's empire until the mid-twentieth century. Spain no longer relies on the slave trade.

4. B: Neither Ecuador nor Paraguay received independence from Spain until 1830. Argentina received independence from Spain in 1810, so A cannot be the correct answer. C is also incorrect because Bolivia became independent from Spain in 1825, and Uruguay followed three years later. Peru gained independence from Spain in 1821, and Brazil was free of Portuguese control by 1822. In 1818, Chile also became independent from Spain; Colombia followed suit the next year. Thus all the other nations listed had received their independence from Spain or Portugal during the previous two decades.

5. D: Ten nations received independence during the first thirty years of the nineteenth century. A is incorrect; the American Revolution was fought during the latter 1770s and early 1780s, some decades before independence movements in South America. In fact, the American Revolution inspired some of the movements. France did not have significant possessions in South America, so B is wrong. Nations

- 58 -

on the west coast were among the last to receive independence, making C incorrect. The landlocked countries of Bolivia and Uruguay were among the last to receive their independence.

6. A: The Mayan Empire collapsed internally, whereas the other civilizations were conquered by the Spanish. The Incan Empire was the last to fall, making B an incorrect choice. None of the empires was located in North America, as the head of the chart makes clear, so C is not valid. The Mayans were not conquered by Spain, as the other two empires were. D is thus incorrect.

7. C: The Spanish conquistadors were active in both Central and South America during the sixteenth century. A is incorrect; Portugal was active in Brazil, but that location is not mentioned in the chart. The Mayan empire is older than both Aztec and Incan civilizations, making B incorrect. There is no indication that the Incan warriors in Peru tried to assist the Aztec of Mexico when they battled the Spanish more than a decade before another conquistador would arrive in Peru.

8. C: He repeats the phrase "save the Union" four times. He explains that slavery is not his primary issue and discusses all the ways he would manipulate that institution to preserve the Union. Lincoln states directly that his object is neither to free the slave nor to destroy slavery, making the first answer incorrect. The second answer, likewise, is incorrect; there is no mention of compensation for the slave owner in this passage. He does not mention winning the war; thus D is not correct.

9. D: In 1848, gold was discovered in California at John Sutter's mill, leading to the migration known as the Forty-Niners. The silver rush in Nevada came later, making A incorrect. The transcontinental railroad was completed in 1869, which is not included in the chart; B is not a viable response. C is also incorrect because the founding of Spanish missions in California and the Southwest had occurred several centuries earlier.

10. D: With an increasing population, cities and towns sprang up and became sites of hotels, brothels, laundries, and saloons. A is not likely; most of the migration consisted of men coming to seek their fortunes and planning to return east. The key term in B is *most*. Although the women who went west often did establish businesses, most of the new migrants were men. The Civil War did not begin until 1860, more than a decade after the Gold Rush. The harsh climate conditions were not the only reason for the deaths that occurred during western migration. In any case, death would not be a contributor to increased population.

11. B: The railroad, which required only 6 to 8 days, offered a 10- to 20-day advantage over all other modes of transporting goods or people. A is an incorrect choice because a steamboat to New Orleans combined with a packet ship to New York required 28 days. The route across the Erie Canal required 18 days, making C also incorrect. The keelboat, used in the earliest part of the nineteenth century, was

only part of the cumbersome 52-day route that required both water and overland travel to reach New York.

12. D: Using keelboat and wagon required 52 days of travel. Combining steamboat, canal, and railroad cut the time by more than 30 days, a larger amount of time saved than any other new development. Steamboat and packet required 28 days of travel, while the railroad took 6 to 8 days, a savings of 20 to 22 days, making answer A incorrect. Likewise, B is wrong; while the canal took 18 days, the railroad took 6 to 8 days, savings 10 to 12 days. The canal route took 18 days while the steamboat and packet required 28 days, thus saving 10 days and making answer C wrong.

13. C: Virginia's plan called for representation based on population, which would work to the advantage of the more populous states. Option A is incorrect; Virginia would not have suggested representation based on wealth if it were a poor state. Response B incorporates the motto of the French Revolution and is irrelevant to the Constitution. Answer D is incorrect because the New Jersey plan did not ask for representation to be based on wealth.

14. B: Britain's Parliament has a two-house system, which may well have been a model for the Virginia Plan. Option A is not correct because the Mayflower Compact set up a more theocratic system of government. Answer C is also wrong; some historians believe that the Iroquois system of government influenced the framers' ideas, but there is no indication that the Sioux system did so. Response D is clearly incorrect because the legislature is not a monarchy.

15. D: The Electoral College was a compromise over the method for electing the president. Choice A is incorrect because wealth has nothing to do with the role of the Electoral College. Response B, likewise, is a false statement; the appointment of Supreme Court justices is not a function of the Electoral College but of the chief executive. Electing senators is also not the responsibility of the Electoral College, making choice C incorrect.

16. C: Young people protested being old enough to fight and die for their country while being denied voting rights. A is incorrect because women had gained the right to vote with passage of the Nineteenth Amendment in 1920. B is also wrong. African American males were guaranteed suffrage following the Civil War; African American females gained the right in 1920. The baby boom ended in 1964, so D is not correct.

17. A: The Nile River flooded regularly and reliably, irrigating the crops of the ancient Egyptians. This best explains the stability of Egyptian culture. Answer B can be rejected because though the Nile River is expansive; its size did not prevent the Egyptian people from settling elsewhere. Answer C can be rejected because the Valley of the Kings, an ancient Egyptian city, did not separate Upper and Lower Egypt. Answer D can be rejected because, even if true, interaction with other

cultures is more likely to lead to a dynamic, changing culture than a stable, unchanging culture.

18. B: Although Charlemagne himself may not have believed his authority was conferred by the Pope, Charlemagne's successors sometimes used the title "Holy Roman Emperor" (given to them by the Pope) as a basis for their authority. Thus, the title "Holy Roman Emperor" strengthened the notion that political authority was conferred by the Pope. Charlemagne united much of Europe under a single ruler prior to being named Holy Roman Emperor. While Catholicism may have been the recognized religion, the naming of Charlemagne as Holy Roman Emperor did not make it so. After being so named, Charlemagne did not renounce his conquests. This eliminates options A, C, and D respectively.

19. B: Johann Gutenberg's printing press led to increased scientific knowledge and advancement as scientific texts were printed and dispersed throughout Europe. Because the distribution of such texts extended outside of Germany, options C and D may be eliminated. Gutenberg Bibles were printed using Gutenberg's press, and thus Gutenberg's invention was likely a factor in the Reformation of the Catholic Church. In fact, Martin Luther's Ninety-Five Theses (against the Catholic Church) were printed using a printing press. However, this reformation occurred alongside, rather than in place of, the advancement of scientific knowledge. This eliminates option A.

20. C: With its emphasis on an individual's relationship with God and personal responsibility for salvation, the religious reformation sparked by Martin Luther in 1517 contributed to a rise in individualism. Rather than weakening the civil authorities in Europe, the Reformation served to strengthen many secular authorities by undermining the authority of the Catholic Church. This eliminates answer B. Although the Reformation deemphasized the Virgin Mary, it influenced improvements to education for women and girls, particularly in Germany. This eliminates answer A. Finally, option D can be rejected because the Catholic Church underwent its own internal reformation, in part due to Luther's Reformation.

21. B: Many Americans migrated during World War II, seeking work in war-related factories; boomtowns sprang up as a result. Some Japanese-Americans served in the United States military during World War II; in fact, the all-Japanese 442nd Regimental Combat Team, was decorated by the U.S. government for its service. This eliminates choice D. Answer C can be rejected because Caucasian and African-American soldiers served in segregated units. Answer A can be eliminated because consumption actually increased in postwar American society, as production was high and returning U.S. soldiers had income to spend.

22. D: The Truman Doctrine was intended to prevent Greece and Turkey from becoming communist countries. However, its broad language had implications beyond those two nations, suggesting that U.S. policy generally should be to aid

people who resisted outside forces attempting to impose communist rule. This doctrine led to U.S. involvement in Korea and Vietnam, where U.S. forces fought against communist forces in those nations. The United States did have a plan for assisting the European economies, but it was the Marshall Plan, not the Truman Doctrine. This eliminates choice B. While President Truman did establish a President's Committee on Civil Rights, it was not as a result of the Truman Doctrine. This eliminates answer A. Finally, when inflation plagued the postwar U.S. economy, the federal government took measures to address inflation and other economic issues, rather than steering clear of them. This eliminates choice C.

23. D: During the Vietnam War, a central aim of the United States was to prevent the spread of communism. At the time of the war, North Vietnamese communist forces threatened South Vietnam, and the United States came to the aid of the South Vietnamese government. The Domino Theory of communism held that one nation's conversion to communism was likely to lead to other nations in that region also converting to communism. The aim of the United States was essentially negative (to stop communism) rather than positive (to implement a specific kind of democracy). This eliminates option A. Option B and C can both be rejected because neither describes the primary aim of U.S. involvement in Vietnam in the 1960s and 1970s. While A, B, and C could have been incidental benefits obtained by fighting North Vietnam, none correctly state the primary goal of the U.S.

24. C: The male passengers of the Mayflower signed the Compact after a disagreement regarding where in the Americas they should establish a colony. The Compact served as a written basis for laws in their subsequent colony. Because the Mayflower Compact did not list particular rights, it is not best understood as a blueprint for the Bill of Rights. This eliminates choice B. Though the Compact did in part serve as a basis for government, it did not declare independence from King James; its last line, for example, specifically refers to King James as the writers' sovereign. This eliminates choice A. Finally, although the Mayflower Compact does include religious language, it is a brief document that does not detail, defend, or establish as official any particular religious doctrine, including Puritan religious doctrine. This eliminates choice D.

25. C: Women, including notable women's rights activists such as Susan B. Anthony, figured importantly in the temperance movement of the 19th century in the United States. Many women were motivated not only by the association of saloons with gambling and prostitution, but by the association of alcohol and domestic violence. Lost productivity was a concern held by figures such as Henry Ford, but figured less prominently with respect to women's role in the temperance movement. This eliminates option B. Option D, infertility, was not a motivating factor. Regarding option A, some women's rights activists were also concerned about race relations and racial injustice, but a specific concern about racial violence was not a primary motivating factor behind the drive for temperance.

26. D: In a parliamentary form of government, the executive branch is essentially a committee of the legislative branch. This is the only answer that correctly describes the relation between the executive branch and another branch of the government. The executive branch is neither a committee of the judicial branch, nor is it appointed by the judicial branch; this eliminates options B and C. The executive branch does not appoint members of the legislative branch; this eliminates option A. In the parliamentary government in Great Britain, for example, the legislature elects the Prime Minister, and the members of the Prime Minister's Cabinet are also selected from members of the legislative branch (either the House of Commons or the House of Lords).

27. C: Inflation is an overall increase in prices. Inflation commonly occurs when there is a large amount of printed currency circulating in an economy at a time when there are few available goods relative to that amount. Options A and B can be eliminated because each describe conditions under which deflation occurs (an overall falling of prices, the opposite of inflation). Option D can be rejected because when there is a relatively low amount of currency circulating within in an economy together with a relatively low number of available goods, prices are not apt to rise.

28. A: Eli Whitney's invention of the cotton gin, a mechanism for quickly separating cotton seeds from cotton fiber, helped elevate cotton as a basis of the Southern economy. Option B can be rejected because, rather than leading to smaller plantations, the invention led to larger cotton plantations. Choice C can be rejected because the United States did not need to import cotton; rather, particularly after the invention of the cotton gin, the United States became a leading exporter of cotton. Finally, option D can be rejected because with larger plantations came an increased need for slaves: the cotton gin had the effect of increasing dependence on slave labor rather than decreasing it.

29. D: Arabic mathematicians, such as the ninth-century mathematician al-Khwarizmi, made important contributions to algebra; the term "algebra" itself derives from a work of al-Khwarizmi's. However, Arabic algebra did not recognize negative numbers; this eliminates option B. Option C can be rejected because probability was developed initially by French mathematicians Blaise Pascal and Pierre de Fermat. Option A can be rejected because modern calculus (building on earlier foundations) is usually taken to have begun (separately) in the works of Isaac Newton and Gottfried Leibniz.

30. A: Jonas Salk's polio vaccine prevented thousands of new cases of polio in a nation which had become accustomed to the ravages of the disease. The invention was a major innovation that affected Americans all over the United States, as children were vaccinated against the disease. Unfortunately, Salk's vaccine did cause polio in a small number of children; however, option B can be rejected because the impact of this was lesser than the impact than the near eradication of the disease in the United States. Option C can be rejected because, although Salk's

manner of announcing the vaccine ruffled the feathers of some of his scientist peers, it did not ignite a widespread or public debate regarding the media and science. Finally, option D can be rejected because it is simply false.

31. D: The Treaty of Tordesillas was between Spain and Portugal. It was executed in 1491, not in the 1500s (a). The treaty did not set up a "Line of Demarcation" (b); this line was previously established 100 leagues west of the Cape Verde Islands by the Pope in response to demands by Ferdinand and Isabella of Spain to confirm their South American colonization. Since the line's division gave more territory to Spain than Portugal, but Portugal had a more powerful navy at the time, Spain and Portugal agreed through the Treaty of Tordesillas to move the Line of Demarcation farther west, not east (c). The treaty was not initiated by the Pope (d); he established the original Line of Demarcation. The treaty moved this line west, and Spain and Portugal agreed to this treaty. .

32. C: Hernando Cortes conquered the Mexican Aztecs in 1519. He had several advantages over the Indians, including horses, armor for his soldiers, and guns. In addition, Cortes' troops unknowingly transmitted smallpox to the Aztecs, which devastated their population as they had no immunity to this foreign illness. Vasco Nunez de Balboa (a) was the first European explorer to view the Pacific Ocean when he crossed the Isthmus of Panama in 1513. Juan Ponce de Leon (b) also visited and claimed Florida in Spain's name in 1513. Cabeza de Vaca (d) was one of only four men out of 400 to return from an expedition led by Panfilio de Narvaez in 1528, and was responsible for spreading the story of the Seven Cities of Cibola (the "cities of gold").

33. B: Hernando de Soto led an expedition of 600 men to southeastern America between 1539 and 1541, getting as far west as Oklahoma and discovering the Mississippi River in the process. Francisco Vasquez de Coronado (a) and his men made an expedition to southwestern America between 1540 and 1542, traveling from Mexico across the Rio Grande and going to New Mexico, Arizona, Texas, Oklahoma, and Kansas. In the process, they became some of the first European explorers to see the Grand Canyon. Hernando Cortes (c) conquered the Aztecs of Mexico in 1519. Juan Ponce de Leon (d) explored Florida looking for the Fountain of Youth and for gold in 1513. At the time, he also claimed Florida for Spain.

34. D: The conquistadores had to deal with labor shortages during their colonization of America in the 16th century. This was attributable to the fact that Spain during this time did not suffer from overpopulation, so only about 200,000 Spaniards migrated to America. To address the shortage of labor, the Spanish first used Indian slaves. Only after the Indians were decimated by diseases brought from Europe and from being overworked did the Spanish begin to import slaves from Africa (b). The first system used by the Spanish was the *encomienda* system of large estates or manors, which was only later succeeded by the *hacienda* system (c), which was similar but not as harsh. It is not true that New Spain's society had no kind of class

system (a). In fact, this society was rigidly divided into three strata. The highest class was Spanish natives (*peninsulares*), the middle class consisted of those born in America to Spanish parents (*creoles*), and the lowest class was made up of Mestizos, or Indians.

35. D: All of these explorers were involved in the search for a Northwest Passage (i.e. a route over water from North America to Asia). Giovannia da Verrazzano (a) of Italy sailed under the French flag in 1524 and went up the coast of America from what is now North Carolina to what is now Maine. John Cabot (b) of Italy, also known as Giovanni Caboto, was commissioned by England to look for a Northwest Passage in 1497, and was the first European to come to North America since the Vikings claimed the land in England's name. Jacques Cartier (c) made three expeditions to America beginning in 1534 on behalf of France. He explored and claimed the St. Lawrence River area, progressing as far as Montreal in Canada.

36. B: King William's War, which was fought between 1689 and1697, included quite a few violent border attacks by Indians in America, but no major army battles. The Treaty of Ryswick ending this war did not make any changes in territories. Queen Anne's War (a), which lasted from 1702 to 1713, was fought against France and Spain. It was ended by the Treaty of Utrecht, which ceded much territory to England. King George's War (c), which lasted from 1739 to 1748, involved major army battles on American soil. American soldiers went on a number of expeditions with British troops. The Treaty of Aix-la-Chapelle ended this war. In it, England returned Louisbourg to France, trading it for territories on the Indian continent. The French and Indian War (d), which lasted from 1754 to 1763, featured many army battles on American soil. The 1763 Treaty of Paris ending this war ceded all of France's territories in Canada and North America to England.

37. D: The person who was not a presidential candidate in the 1824 election was John C. Calhoun. When John Quincy Adams was elected, Calhoun became his Vice President, but he had not run for President. Henry Clay (a) was Speaker of the House at the time, and ran for President with the "American System" as his platform. He was the only candidate to present an actual program for voters' consideration. Georgia's William H. Crawford (b) was Secretary of the Treasury at the time, and he was the choice for candidate by Congress's caucus. John Quincy Adams (c) was Secretary of State then, and this office historically tended to lead to the presidency. Tennessee's Andrew Jackson ran based on his military victories in the War of 1812. Note: Jackson won 43% of the popular vote, but only 38% of the electoral vote due to the presence of four candidates. The House of Representatives voted on the three top candidates, eliminating Henry Clay. Clay gave his support to John Quincy Adams, who returned the favor by appointing Clay Secretary of State. Jackson and his followers criticized this as corrupt deal making, and used this claim as the basis for their campaign for the next election in 1828.

38. B: The area of reform that may be said to have met with the most difficulty in its early years is free public schools. The first reformers, such as Horace Mann and Henry Barnard, encountered apathy or resistance in their crusade to establish free public schools. Even though this movement gained momentum during the 1830s, there were still very few public schools in the Western states, even fewer in the Southern states, and none at all for blacks in the South. The movement for higher education (a) had some better early success thanks to a few innovations. The first state-funded women's college, Troy Female Seminary, was founded in 1839 in Troy, New York. In Ohio, Oberlin College became the first co-educational college in the country. In Watertown, Boston, the Perkins School for the Blind was the first school for the blind in the country. In 1887, Anne Sullivan, a graduate of Perkins, was sent by Perkins's director Michael Anagnos to Alabama to teach Helen Keller. She returned to the school with Helen Keller the following year. The area of mental institutions (c) experienced innovation in the form of campaigns to treat mentally ill people more humanely in hospitals designed for that purpose. Dorothea Dix was the most prominent leader in this crusade. Prison reform (d) experienced innovation in the form of building new penitentiaries intended to rehabilitate criminals rather than to simply punish them. The first new penitentiary was built in 1821 in Auburn, New York. The abolitionist movement saw innovations through the work of William Lloyd Garrison, who began his paper *The Liberator* in 1831, founded the New England Anti-Slavery Society in 1832 and the American Anti-Slavery Society in 1833, and advocated immediate and complete emancipation, enlivening the abolitionist movement. Theodore Weld was also an abolitionist who proposed a slower emancipation, and escaped slave Frederick Douglass became an abolitionist orator and published the *North Star* newspaper. Many novels, such as Harriet Beecher Stowe's *Uncle Tom's Cabin,* also lent support to this movement. Another movement that saw innovations in this era of social reform was the feminist movement.

39. D: All of these (D) factors helped the Republicans gain control of both the House and the Senate in 1994 during Clinton's administration. Allegations regarding the President's character, specifically involvement in the Whitewater Development Corporation scandal and allegations of inappropriate sexual advances made by Clinton during his gubernatorial tenure, (a) and (b) were factors that weakened the Democratic position.   Additionally, disagreements regarding healthcare legislation and gays in the military (c) further weakened the President's credibility and strengthened the Republican position.

40. C: The rates of both productivity and inflation in the US was approximately 2% by 2000. By this time, the US economy was not increasing at a rate of 5% a year (a) but of 4% a year. Almost half of industrial growth contributing to economic prosperity was due to the "information revolution" made possible by the invention of the PC. The rate of unemployment in America at this time had not gone down to 6% (b) but to 4.7%. The stock market in the US had not just doubled in six years (d); it had actually quadrupled from 1992-1998 due to the increase in American

households that owned stocks or bonds. Most of this ownership resulted from tax law changes regulating retirement accounts. In the 1998 fiscal year, the federal government did have a surplus; the surplus that year was $70 billion, and additional surpluses were predicted for the future.

Practice Test #2

English

Questions 1–5 refer to the following passage:

Who Was This Man?

"You have a visitor, you see," said Monsieur Defarge.

"What did you say?"

"Here is a visitor."

The shoemaker looked up as before, but without removing a hand from his work.

"Come!" said Defarge. "Here is monsieur, who knows a well-made shoe when he sees one. Show him that shoe you are working at. Take it, monsieur."

Mr. Lorry took it in his hand.

"Tell monsieur what kind of shoe it is, and the maker's name."

There was a longer pause than usual, before the shoemaker replied: "I forget what it was you asked me. What did you say?"

"I said, couldn't you describe the kind of shoe, for monsieur's information?"

"It is a lady's shoe. It is a young lady's walking-shoe. It is in the present mode. I never saw the mode. I have had a pattern in my hand."

He glanced at the shoe with some little passing touch of pride.

"And the maker's name?" said Defarge.

Now that he had no work to hold, he laid the knuckles of the right hand in the hollow of the left, and then the knuckles of the left hand in the hollow of the right, and then passed a hand across his bearded chin, and so on in regular changes, without a moment's intermission. The task of recalling him from the vagrancy into which he always sank when he had spoken, was like recalling some very weak person from a swoon, or endeavouring, in the hope of some disclosure, to stay the spirit of a fast-dying man.

"Did you ask me for my name?"

"Assuredly I did."

"One Hundred and Five, North Tower."

"Is that all?"

"One Hundred and Five, North Tower."

With a weary sound that was not a sigh, nor a groan, he bent to work again, until the silence was again broken.

"You are not a shoemaker by trade?" said Mr. Lorry, looking steadfastly at him.

His haggard eyes turned to Defarge as if he would have transferred the question to him: but as no help came from that quarter, they turned back on the questioner when they had sought the ground.

"I am not a shoemaker by trade? No, I was not a shoemaker by trade. I-I learnt it here. I taught myself. I asked leave to ... "

He lapsed away, even for minutes, ringing those measured changes on his hands the whole time. His eyes came slowly back, at last, to the face from which they had wandered; when they rested on it, he started, and resumed, in the manner of a sleeper that moment awake, reverting to a subject of last night.

"I asked leave to teach myself, and I got it with much difficulty after a long while, and I have made shoes ever since."

—Excerpted from *A Tale of Two Cities* by Charles Dickens

1. Monsieur Defarge and Mr. Lorry are visiting
    a. an art gallery in Paris.
    b. a man who has been ill.
    c. a member of the British government.
    d. a doctor making hospital calls.

2. Based on the name he gives, the reader can infer that the man
    a. has spent time in a prison tower.
    b. has been traveling throughout Europe.
    c. has been homeless a long time.
    d. first left home as a young man.

3. Which of the following is NOT a sign of the man's mental condition?
    a. his inability to complete a thought
    b. his identifying himself by a location instead of a name
    c. the repetitive motion of his hands
    d. his cheerful laughter

4. The man has asked to learn the trade of
    a. woodcarving.
    b. glassblowing.
    c. blacksmithing.
    d. shoemaking.

5. What can the reader infer about the identity of Monsieur Defarge?
    a. He is the unkind jailer at the prison.
    b. He is a friend keeping the man safe.
    c. He is the man's loving son or grandson.
    d. He is a cruel doctor in a hospital.

Questions 6–10 refer to the following selection:
Why Has He Come?

He had returned in early spring. It was autumn before he found her.

A quiet college town in the hills, a broad, shady street, a pleasant house standing in its own lawn, with trees and flowers about it. He had the address in his hand, and the number showed clear on the white gate. He walked up the straight gravel path and rang the bell. And elderly servant opened the door.

"Does Mrs. Morroner live here?'

"No, sir."

"This is number twenty-eight?

"Yes, sir."

"Who does live here?"

"Miss Wheeling, sir."

Ah! Her maiden name. They had told him, but he had forgotten.

He stepped inside. "I would like to see her," he said.

He was ushered into a still parlor, cool and sweet with the scent of flowers, the flowers she had always loved best. It almost brought tears to his eyes. All their years of happiness rose in his mind again—the exquisite beginnings; the days of eager longing before she was really his; the deep, still beauty of her love.

Surely she would forgive him—she must forgive him. He would humble himself; he would tell her of his honest remorse—his absolute determination to be a different man.

Through the wide doorway there came in to him two women. One like a tall Madonna, bearing a baby in her arms.

Marion, calm, steady, definitely impersonal, nothing but a clear pallor to hint of inner stress.

Gerta, holding the child as a bulwark, with a new intelligence in her face, and her blue, adoring eyes fixed on her friend—not upon him.

He looked from one to the other dumbly.

And the woman who had been his wife asked quietly:

"What have you to say to us?"

- selection from Turned by Charlotte Perkins Gilman

6. The man is looking for a woman so that he can
   a. propose marriage to her.
   b. invite her to a party.
   c. ask for forgiveness.
   d. hire her as a governess.

7. What effect does the description of the setting suggest?
    a. This is an orderly, peaceful, and lovely spot.
    b. A storm is coming, and the wind is increasing.
    c. The sea is nearby, and the waves are crashing.
    d. Great changes are about to take place.

8. What conclusion can the reader draw about the child being carried by the tall woman, Gerta?
    a. The home is an orphanage.
    b. The child belongs to the man and his wife.
    c. The child is not well and the man has come as the doctor.
    d. The man has fathered the child and been unfaithful to his wife.

9. What symbol is used to represent the man's former happiness?
    a. the woman's maiden name
    b. flowers
    c. Madonna
    d. the wide doorway

10. Marion is not as unaffected as she tries to be when the man visits. The reader can infer that fact from
    a. her fear of seeing the man alone.
    b. her refusal to see the man.
    c. her pale face.
    d. her kind words to the man.

Questions 11–18 refer to the following selection:

VISUAL PERCEPTION

It is tempting to think that your eyes are simply mirrors that reflect whatever is in front of them. Researchers, however, have shown that your brain is constantly working to create the impression of a continuous, uninterrupted world.

For instance, in the last ten minutes, you have blinked your eyes around 200 times. You have probably not been aware of any of these interruptions in your visual world. Something you probably have not seen in a long time without the aid of a mirror is your nose. It is always right there, down in the bottom corner of your vision, but your brain filters it out so that you are not aware of your nose unless you purposefully look at it.

Nor are you aware of the artery that runs right down the middle of your retina. It creates a large blind spot in your visual field, but you never notice the hole it leaves. To see this blind spot, try the following: Cover your left eye with your hand. With your right eye, look at the O on the left. As you move your head closer to the O, the X will disappear as it enters the blind spot caused by your optical nerve.

O   X

Your brain works hard to make the world look continuous!

11. The word filters, as used in this passage, most nearly means:
    a. Alternates
    b. Reverses
    c. Ignores
    d. Depends

12. The word retina, as used in this passage, most nearly means:
    a. Optical illusion
    b. Part of the eye
    c. Pattern
    d. Blindness

13. Which of the following statements can be inferred from this passage?
    a. Not all animals' brains filter out information.
    b. Visual perception is not a passive process.
    c. Blind spots cause accidents.
    d. The eyes never reflect reality.

14. What is the author's purpose for including the two letters in the middle of the passage?
    a. To demonstrate the blind spot in the visual field.
    b. To organize the passage.
    c. To transition between the last two paragraphs of the passage.
    d. To prove that the blind spot is not real.

15. What is the main purpose of this passage?
    a. To persuade the reader to pay close attention to blind spots.
    b. To explain the way visual perception works.
    c. To persuade the reader to consult an optometrist if the O and X disappear.
    d. To prove that vision is a passive process.

16. Based on the passage, which of the following statements is true?
    a. The brain cannot accurately reflect reality.
    b. Glasses correct the blind spot caused by the optical nerve.
    c. Vision is the least important sense.
    d. The brain fills in gaps in the visual field.

17. The author mentions the nose to illustrate what point?
    a. The brain filters out some visual information.
    b. Not all senses work the same way.
    c. Perception is a passive process.
    d. The sense of smell filters out information.

18. Which of the following statements can be inferred from the second paragraph?
    a. The brain filters out the sound created by the shape of the ears.
    b. The brain does not perceive all activity in the visual field.
    c. Closing one eye affects depth perception.
    d. The brain evolved as a result of environmental factors.

Questions 19–27 refer to the following selection:

EARLY POLITICAL PARTIES
The United States has always been a pluralistic society, meaning it has always embraced many points of view and many groups with different identities. That is not to say that these groups have always seen eye to eye. The first political parties developed in the United States as a result of conflicting visions of the American identity. Many politicians believed that wealthy merchants and lawyers represented the country's true identity, but many others saw it in the farmers and workers who formed the country's economic base.
The event that brought this disagreement to the surface was the creation of the Bank of the United States in 1791. The bank set out to rid the country of the debts it had accumulated during the American

- 73 -

Revolution. Until then, each state was responsible for its own debts. The Bank of the United States, however, wanted to assume these debts and pay them off itself. While many people considered this offer to be a good financial deal for the states, many states were uncomfortable with the arrangement because they saw it as a power play by the federal government. If a central bank had control over the finances of individual states, the people who owned the bank would profit from the states in the future. This concern was the basis of the disagreement: Who should have more power, the individual states or the central government?

The Democratic-Republican Party developed to protest the bank, but it came to represent a vision of America with power spread among states. The Federalist Party was established in defense of the bank, but its ultimate vision was of a strong central government that could help steer the United States toward a more competitive position in the world economy.

These different points of view—central government versus separate states—would not be resolved easily. These same disagreements fueled the tension that erupted into the Civil War over half a century later.

19. According to the passage, the word "pluralistic" most nearly means:
    a. Divisive
    b. Conservative
    c. Tolerant
    d. Liberty

20. What is the author's purpose in writing this passage?
    a. To persuade the reader to accept the Federalist Party's point of view.
    b. To explain the disagreements between early American political parties.
    c. To explain the importance of a strong central government.
    d. To criticize the founders of the Bank of the United States.

21. The word "competitive" is used in the passage to mean:
    a. Inferior
    b. Stronger
    c. Partisan
    d. Identity

22. Which of the following best describes the main idea of the passage?
    a. Political parties should emphasize areas of agreement instead of disagreement.
    b. The earliest political parties in the U.S. reflected conflicting interests.
    c. The Federalist Party had a better plan for the America's interests abroad.
    d. The Bank of the United States was not a secure financial institution.

23. In the last sentence of the first paragraph, the pronoun "it" refers to which of the following?
  a. The country's identity.
  b. The future of the country.
  c. State's rights.
  d. A political party.

24. Which of the following statements can be inferred from the second paragraph?
  a. The formation of the Bank of the United States should not have created so much conflict.
  b. Individual states believed that they should not have to share their profits with the central government.
  c. The bank was attempting to swindle the states.
  d. The states were not willing to listen to reason.

25. Which of the following statements best fits with the viewpoint of the Federalist Party?
  a. The U.S. should be a confederacy of individual states with equal power.
  b. The government should not meddle in the affairs of states.
  c. States should not have any rights.
  d. The stronger the central government, the stronger the country.

26. Which of the following statements best fits with the viewpoint of the Democratic-Republican Party?
  a. The federal government should not have too much power.
  b. The Bank of the United States would never be able to repay the states' debts.
  c. The states should not have too much power.
  d. The constitution must be revised to give the government more power.

27. Which of the following statements can be inferred from the final paragraph?
  a. The Civil War was fought between the Federalist and the Democratic-Republican Parties.
  b. The different interests reflected by the first two political parties were not easily reconciled.
  c. The Civil War could have been avoided if the Bank of the United States had not been created.
  d. The Bank of the United States is a direct cause of the Civil War.

Identify the sentence that contains an error in usage, punctuation or grammar. If there are no errors, choose answer choice "d."

28.
    a. Fear of the number thirteen is called "triskaidekaphobia."
    b. The earwig's name originates in the myth that the insect burrows into the human ear to lay its eggs.
    c. The longest word recorded in an English dictionary are "Pneumonoultramicroscopicsilicovolcanokoniosis."
    d. No mistake.

29.
    a. "Stewardesses," "desegregated," and "reverberated" are the longest words a person can type using only his or her left hand.
    b. The largest catfish ever catch is 646 pounds, the size of an adult brown bear.
    c. A flyswatter has holes in it to reduce air resistance.
    d. No mistake.

30.
    a. The canoe cut a clear swath through the algae.
    b. Though widely ridiculed when first proposed, Alfred Wegener's theory of plate tectonics is now an accepted explanation of how continents are formed.
    c. Though a highly influentially anthropologist, Claude Levi-Strauss often took criticism for spending little time in the field studying real cultures.
    d. No mistake.

31.
    a. Fiction writer David Foster Wallace, author of the influential novel Infinite Jest, also authored a book surveying all of the significant theories of infinity in the history of mathematics.
    b. The photograph made the Eiffel Tower look like it was balanced on Oswald's palm.
    c. It is easy to get confused when calculating time differences between time zones a useful way to remember them is that the Atlantic Ocean starts with A, as in A.M., and the Pacific Ocean starts with P, as in P.M.
    d. No mistake.

Choose the sentence that contains a spelling error. If there are no errors, choose answer choice "d."

32.
    a. My favorite Beatles' record is Revolver.
    b. My favorite Beatles' song is "Strawberry Fields"
    c. My favorite Beatle is John Lennon.
    d. No mistake.

33.

    a. I had to have a tooth pulled after a bike accident.
    b. When I received the dentist's bill, I was disgruntled.
    c. I was graitful that I couldn't feel a thing.
    d. No mistake.

34.

    a. Mrs. Albom, the music teacher, financed her summer vacation by bagging groceries at Wal-Mart after school.
    b. We put down a tarp and shook the branches to get the mulberries.
    c. The citric acid used in Vitamin C tablets makes them taste sower.
    d. No mistake.

35.

    a. Despite being born a slave, Benjamin Banneker went on to play a pivotal role in the planning of Washington D. C.
    b. Andrew Johnson is the only president to serve as a sinator after his time as president, which is ironic because the senate had attempted to impeach him when he was president.
    c. The St. Burchardi Church in Halberstadt, Germany, is currently performing a composition by John Cage entitled "As Slow as Possible," a piece that takes 639 years to complete.
    d. No mistake.

36. Where should the following sentence be placed in the paragraph below?

Many people have proposed explanations for this drop.

    1] Surveys of criminal activity in the United States have shown that the 1990s marked a significant drop in crimes such as vehicle theft, rape, and murder. 2] Economist Rick Nevin argues that one contributing factor is the ban on lead gasoline in the 70s because lead poisoning in children has been linked with criminal behavior later in life. 3] Other theories include the controversial claim that legalizing abortion has led to fewer unwanted children and, as a result, fewer potential criminals. 4] Some politicians, including Rudy Giuliani, even take personal responsibility, identifying their policies as effective deterrents to crime.

    a. After sentence 1
    b. After sentence 2
    c. After sentence 3
    d. After sentence 4

37. Where should the following sentence be placed in the paragraph below?

Insects that carry the disease can develop resistance to the chemicals, or insecticides, that are used to kill the mosquitoes.

> 1] Malaria, a disease spread by insects and parasites, has long proven to be difficult to treat. 2] Part of the explanation has to do with adaptation, or the ability of one generation to pass its strengths on to another. 3] Some insects are simply not affected by these insecticides. 4] Unfortunately, these are the insects that survive and go on to reproduce, creating another generation of insects that are immune to the current insecticides. 5] Many researchers have abandoned hope for insecticides as a cure for malaria, turning their attention instead to other forms of defense, such as protein-blockers that protect humans from the effects of the disease instead of from the carriers.

a. After sentence 1
b. After sentence 2
c. After sentence 3
d. After sentence 4

38. Choose the sentence that is correct and most clearly written.
a. The novelist David Markson is known for his experimental works, such as "This Is Not a Novel."
b. Experimental works such as "This Is Not a Novel" have been wrote by David Markson.
c. Novelist David Markson is knew for his experimental works, such as "This Is Not a Novel."
d. David Markson is a novelist who is known for experimentation his works include "This Is Not a Novel."

39. Choose the sentence that is correct and most clearly written.
a. I intended to mow the yard, but I wanted to wait until evening when it are cooler.
b. I intended to mow the yard, but I wanted to wait until evening when it would be cooler.
c. I intended to mow the yard, but not until it getting cooler in the evening.
d. I intended to mow the yard, but I waits until evening when it was cooler.

40. Choose the sentence that is correct and most clearly written.
   a. We used to dump our lawn clippings, but now we compost them for the garden.
   b. Dumping our lawn clippings used to be something done by us, but now composting is done by us for the garden.
   c. We used to dumps our lawn clippings, but now we composts them for the garden.
   d. We used to dump our lawn clippings, but now I compost them for the garden.

Writing Prompt

Although elementary education proposals have typically emphasized math and science, there is a growing movement to restore fine arts education in the early grades. Many education experts assert that neglecting music, dance, and painting produces students who have a great deal of knowledge but little capability of expression. Furthermore, they argue, the creativity and free-thinking required for the practice of the fine arts leads to innovation and progress in other areas. Critics of these proposals argue that the United States still lags behind other countries in science and mathematics test scores, and should focus on improving performance in these areas before allocating extra funds to arts programs.

In an organized, coherent, and supported essay explain what you think the education system should do and why it should do so. Address the pros and cons.

Mathematics

1. Two even integers and one odd integer are multiplied together. Which of the following could be their product?
    a. 3.75
    b. 9
    c. 16.2
    d. 24

2. If $520 \div x = 40n$, then which of the following is equal to nx?
    a. 13
    b. 40nx
    c. 26
    d. 40

3. In Figure 2 (pictured below), angles b and d are equal. What is the degree measure of angle d?

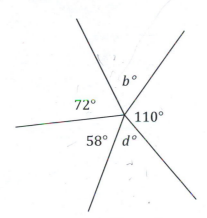

Figure 2

    a. 240°
    b. 120°
    c. 80°
    d. 60°

4. Janice weighs x pounds. Elaina weighs 23 pounds more than Janice. June weighs 14 pounds more than Janice. In terms of x, what is the sum of their weights minus 25 pounds?
    a. 3x + 37
    b. 3x + 12
    c. x + 12
    d. 3x – 25

5. A bag contains 14 blue, 6 red, 12 green and 8 purple buttons. 25 buttons are removed from the bag randomly. How many of the removed buttons were red if the chance of drawing a red button from the bag is now 1/3?
  a. 0
  b. 1
  c. 3
  d. 5

6. There are 80 mg / 0.8 ml in Acetaminophen Concentrated Infant Drops. If the proper dosage for a four year old child is 240 mg, how many milliliters should the child receive?
  a. 0.8 ml
  b. 1.6 ml
  c. 2.4 ml
  d. 3.2 ml

7. Solve the following equation: $(y + 1)(y + 2)(y + 3)$
  a. $y^2 + 3y + 2$
  b. $3y^2 + 6y + 3$
  c. $2y^2 + 11y$
  d. $y^3 + 6y^2 + 11y + 6$

8. What is the area of the parallelogram in the figure below?

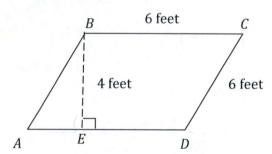

  a. 144 square feet
  b. 12 square feet
  c. 36 square feet
  d. 24 square feet

9. 90 students are enrolled in English or Math or both. 50 students are enrolled in both English and Math. If 25 students are enrolled in English, but not Math, how many students are enrolled in Math but not English?
  a. 15
  b. 25
  c. 50
  d. 65

10. If a savings account earns 3.75% simple interest each month, how much interest will a deposit of $2,500 earn in one month?
  a. $93.75
  b. $666.67
  c. $2,503.75
  d. $2,593.75

11. A regular toilet uses 3.2 gallons of water per flush. A low flow toilet uses 1.6 gallons of water per flush. What is the difference between the number of gallons used by the regular toilet and the low flow toilet after 375 flushes?
  a. 100 gallons
  b. 525 gallons
  c. 600 gallons
  d. 1,200 gallons

12. Five dice are rolled together one time. What is the probability of rolling five 6s?
  a. $^1/_6$
  b. $^1/_{30}$
  c. $^5/_6$
  d. $^1/_{7,776}$

13. Simplify the following equation: $4(6 - 3)^2 - (-2)$
  a. 34
  b. 38
  c. 42
  d. 48

14. In the figure below, find the value of x:

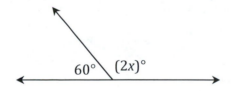

  a. 30
  b. 60
  c. 100
  d. 120

15. In the number 6,502,104.9738, what digit is in the thousandths place?
  a. 3
  b. 5
  c. 6
  d. 8

16. Solve for *n* in the following equation: $4n - p = 3r$
    a. 3r/4 - p
    b. p + 3r
    c. p - 3r
    d. 3r/4 + p/4

17. A square and an equilateral triangle have the same perimeter. If one side of the triangle measures 4 inches, how long is one side of the square?
    a. 10
    b. 8
    c. 6
    d. 3

18. Find the value of *x* in the figure below:

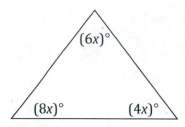

    a. 10
    b. 16
    c. 18
    d. 60

19. What is a good estimate of the circumference of the circle shown below?

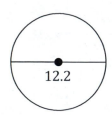

    a. 6
    b. 12
    c. 24
    d. 36

20. Paula received scores of 88, 84, and 91 on her last three math tests. What must she score on her fourth test to average 90% for all four of the tests?
    a. 97
    b. 96
    c. 95
    d. 94

21. What is the product of four squared and six?
    a. 22
    b. 28
    c. 55
    d. 96

22. Solve the following equation: $(y + 2)(y + 3)(y + 4)$
    a. $y^2 + 3y + 2$
    b. $3y^2 + 6y + 3$
    c. $y^3 + 9y^2 + 26y + 24$
    d. $8y^3 + 6y + 8$

23. If one side of a square has a length of 56 cm, what is its perimeter?
    a. 112 cm
    b. 224 cm
    c. 448 cm
    d. 3136 cm

24. $5(80 / 8) + (7 – 2) – (9 \times 5) =$
    a. -150
    b. 10
    c. 100
    d. 230

25. $9x – 3y + 8xy – 3$
If $x = 10$ and $y = -2$, what is the value of this expression?
    a. -67
    b. -61
    c. -79
    d. 241

26. Simplify the following: $9x (3x^2 + 2x - 9)$
    a. $27x^2 + 18x - 81$
    b. $27x^3 + 18x^2 – 81x$
    c. $12x^3 + 11x^2 - x$
    d. $27x^3 + 18x^2 – 18x$

27. Evaluate the following expression, if $x = 3$ and $y = 27$.
$x^5x^2 + y^0 =$
   a. 59,049
   b. 59,050
   c. 2,187
   d. 2,188

28. If x represents the number of students that paid \$100 for a new textbook and y represents the number of students that paid \$50 for a used textbook, which of the following represents the total amount that was spent on used textbooks?
   a. $150y$
   b. $100x$
   c. $50y$
   d. $50x$

29. In the following inequality, solve for x.
$-4x + 8 \geq 48$
   a. $x \geq 10$
   b. $x \geq -10$
   c. $x \leq 10$
   d. $x \leq -10$

30. $x^2 + 12x + 36 = 0$
What is the value of x?
   a. $x = 6$
   b. $x = -6$
   c. $x = 6, -6$
   d. $x = 0, 6$

31. Simplify the following expression.
$$\frac{64x^4 + 8x^3 - 4x^2 + 16x}{8x}$$
   a. $56x^3 - 12x^2 + 8$
   b. $8x^3 + x^2 - x/2 + 2$
   c. $8x^4 + x^3 - x^2/2 + 2x$
   d. $8x^3 + x^2 - 2x + 2$

32. Factor the following expression.
$9x^2y - 18xy - 27y$
   a. $9(x^2y - 2xy - 3y)$
   b. $9y(x + 3)(x + 1)$
   c. $9y(x - 3)(x+1)$
   d. $9y(x + 3)(x - 1)$

33. Simplify the following expression.

$\sqrt{3}(5\sqrt{3} - \sqrt{12} + \sqrt{10})$

    a. $9 + \sqrt{30}$

    b. $15 - \sqrt{15} + \sqrt{13}$

    c. $15\sqrt{3} - 3\sqrt{12} + 3\sqrt{10}$

    d. $3 - \sqrt{13}$

34. $25x - 12x + 6x - 27 = 35$

Solve for x.

    a. $x = 0.42$

    b. $x = 1.44$

    c. $x = 3.26$

    d. $x = 5.23$

35. $(y + 10)^2 - 625 = 0$

Solve for y.

    a. $y = 615$

    b. $y = -15, 15$

    c. $y = -15$

    d. $y = 15, -35$

36. Solve for y using the following system of equations.

$2x - 6y = 12$

$-6x + 14y = 42$

    a. -19.5

    b. -52.5

    c. -2.44

    d. 6.56

37. If $6x + 2x - 26 = -5x$, then $[(2x-1)/7]^3 =$

    a. 0.0787

    b. 0.192

    c. 1.29

    d. 12.7

38. A line passes through points A (-3, 18) and B (5, 2). What is the slope of the line?

    a. 2

    b. -2

    c. 1/2

    d. -1/2

39. Which of the following lines is perpendicular to the line $y = -5x + 27$?
    a. $y = 5x + 27$
    b. $y = -x/5 + 27$
    c. $y = x/5 + 27$
    d. $y = -x/5 - 27$

40. What is the midpoint of points A (-20, 8) and B (5, 3)?
    a. (5.5, 7.5)
    b. (7.5, 5.5)
    c. (5.5, -7.5)
    d. (-7.5, 5.5)

Science

For Questions 1-8 use the following passage and diagram:

Blood consists of a liquid called *plasma*, in which many different types of blood cells are suspended. The plasma also contains many dissolved proteins. These proteins may be studied by subjecting the plasma to *electrophoresis,* in which it is subjected to an electric field, which pulls the proteins through a porous gel. Proteins typically have a negative charge on their surface, so they move toward the anode (positive electrode) in an electric field. The gel acts as a molecular sieve: it interferes with the movement, or *migration*, of the larger proteins more than the small ones, allowing the proteins to be separated on the basis of size. The further the proteins move during the experiment, the smaller they must be.

The experiment results in an *electropherogram*, such as the one shown in the figure below. This is a plot, or graph, of protein concentration versus migration, and corresponds to a graph of concentration versus size. Concentration is measured by passing light of a certain wavelength through the gel: proteins absorb the light, and the resulting *absorbance* measurement is proportional to protein concentration. Many major blood component proteins, such as albumin and several identified by Greek letters, have been discovered in this way. When disease is present, some component proteins may break down into smaller fragments. Others may aggregate, or clump together, to form larger fragments. This results in a change in the electropherogram: new species, corresponding to the aggregates or breakdown products, may be present, and the sizes of the normal peaks may be changed as the concentration of normal products is altered.

The Figure shows an electropherogram from a sick patient with an abnormal component in her blood (arrow). Peaks corresponding to some normal plasma proteins have been labeled. Please examine the electropherogram and answer the following questions.

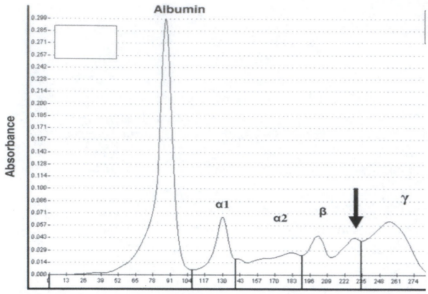

1. Which blood component protein is present in the greatest amounts in the plasma?
   a. Albumin
   b. $\alpha 1$
   c. $\alpha 2$
   d. β

2. Which of the following is the fastest-moving component in the electropherogram?
   a. Albumin
   b. $\alpha 1$
   c. $\alpha 2$
   d. γ

3. Which of the following statements is true about component $\alpha 1$?
   a. The molecules move through the gel faster than those of component $\alpha 2$, but slower than Albumin.
   b. The molecules are larger than albumin, but smaller than all the other components.
   c. The molecules are smaller than albumin, but larger than all the other components.
   d. It is not a protein.

4. Which of the components identified on the electropherogram is the smallest molecule?
   a. Albumin
   b. $\alpha 1$
   c. $\alpha 2$
   d. γ

- 89 -

5. Which of the following is true of the unknown component identified by the arrow?

    a. The molecules are larger than the β component, but smaller than albumin

    b. The molecules are larger than the β component, but smaller than the γ component.

    c. The molecules move more slowly in the gel than all the other components except one.

    d. The molecules move more rapidly in the gel than all the other components except one.

6. Which of the following may be true of the unknown component identified by the arrow?

    a. It is formed of albumin molecules that have aggregated.

    b. It is formed of $\alpha 1$ molecules that have aggregated.

    c. It is formed of $\alpha 2$ molecules that have aggregated.

    d. It is formed of γ molecules that have aggregated.

7. Which of the following may not be true of the unknown component identified by the arrow?

    a. It is formed of albumin molecules that have broken down into fragments.

    b. It is formed of $\alpha 1$ molecules that have broken down into fragments.

    c. It is formed of $\alpha 2$ molecules that have broken down into fragments.

    d. It is formed of γ molecules that have broken down into fragments.

8. The blood of healthy individuals does not contain the unknown component indicated by the arrow. The experiment therefore proves

    a. The unknown component causes the patient's sickness.

    b. The unknown component results from the patient's sickness.

    c. The more of the unknown component there is, the sicker the patient will be.

    d. None of the above.

For Questions 9-16 use the following passage and diagram:

> In a study performed to determine the migration patterns of fish, 34,000 juvenile sablefish of the species *Anoplopoma fimbria* were tagged and released into waters of the eastern Gulf of Alaska during a twenty-year period. The tagged fish were all juveniles (less than 2 years of age), so that the age of the recovered fish could be determined from the date on the tag. This allowed age-specific movement patterns to be studied. Tagged fish were recovered from sites in the Bering Sea, throughout the Gulf of Alaska, and off the coast of British Columbia. The fish were recovered by commercial fishermen, with the results reported to the scientists performing the study. A total of 2011 tagged fish were recovered. It was found that fish spawned in coastal waters move to deeper waters when they are

older. At the same time, they migrate north and west, across the Gulf of Alaska toward the Aleutian Islands. Eventually, they return to the eastern Gulf as adults.

The figure shows tag recoveries from sablefish tagged as juveniles by age (in years) and by depth (in meters) for all the areas in the study. The size of each circle is proportional to the number of recoveries. The range for each data point is 1 to 57 recoveries. The symbol x represents the median age.

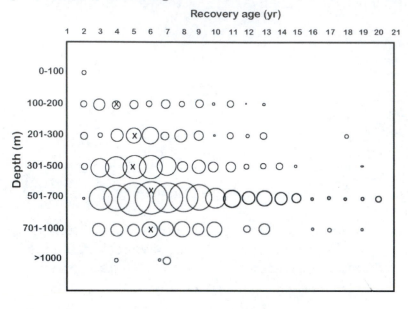

9. If a circle in the graph is twice the size (area) of another circle, this indicates that:
   a. It represents twice as many fish.
   b. The fish it represents were twice as old.
   c. The fish it represents were recovered at twice the depth.
   d. Both A and B.

10. The greatest number of tagged fish were recovered at depths of
    a. 101 – 200 m.
    b. 201 – 300 m.
    c. 301 – 500 m.
    d. 501 – 700 m.

11. What percentage of the released, tagged fish were recovered for this study?
    a. 2011
    b. 20
    c. 6
    d. 17

12. The median age of tagged fish recovered at depths between 301 and 500 meters is approximately
    a. 2 years.
    b. 5 years.
    c. 9 years.
    d. < 2 years.

13. Not all the tagged fish were recovered in this study. Which of the following reasons may be responsible for the losses?
    a. Some fish died during the study.
    b. Some tagged fish were not caught by commercial fishermen during the study.
    c. The tags fell off some of the fish during the study.
    d. All of the above.
14. The largest fish are found at depths of
    a. 101 – 200 m.
    b. 201 – 300 m.
    c. 301 – 500 m.
    d. Can't determine from the data given.

15. Which of the following statements is supported by the data in the figure?
    a. Fish return to the eastern Gulf of Alaska to spawn.
    b. Sablefish move progressively deeper with age.
    c. Sablefish prefer cold waters.
    d. Younger fish swim faster than older ones.

16. The data indicate that sablefish may live as long as
    a. 10 years.
    b. 30 years.
    c. 20 years.
    d. 5 years.

17. Which of the following is not a product of the Krebs cycle?
    a. carbon dioxide
    b. oxygen
    c. adenosine triphosphate (ATP)
    d. energy carriers

18. What kind of bond connects sugar and phosphate in DNA?
    a. hydrogen
    b. ionic
    c. covalent
    d. overt

19. What is the second part of an organism's scientific name?
    a. species
    b. phylum
    c. population
    d. kingdom

20. How are lipids different than other organic molecules?
    a. They are indivisible.
    b. They are not water soluble.
    c. They contain zinc.
    d. They form long proteins.

21. Which of the following is not a steroid?
    a. cholesterol
    b. estrogen
    c. testosterone
    d. hemoglobin

22. Which of the following properties is responsible for the passage of water through a plant?
    a. cohesion
    b. adhesion
    c. osmosis
    d. evaporation

23. Which hormone is produced by the pineal gland?
    a. insulin
    b. testosterone
    c. melatonin
    d. epinephrine

24. What is the name of the organelle that organizes protein synthesis?
    a. mitochondrion
    b. nucleus
    c. ribosome
    d. vacuole

25. Which of the following does not exist as a diatomic molecule?
    a. boron
    b. fluorine
    c. oxygen
    d. nitrogen

26. What is another name for aqueous HI?
    a. hydroiodate acid
    b. hydrogen monoiodide
    c. hydrogen iodide
    d. hydriodic acid

27. Which of the following could be an empirical formula?
    a. C4H8
    b. C2H6
    c. CH
    d. C3H6

28. What is the name for the reactant that is entirely consumed by the reaction?
    a. limiting reactant
    b. reducing agent
    c. reaction intermediate
    d. reagent

29. What is the name for the horizontal rows of the periodic table?
    a. groups
    b. periods
    c. families
    d. sets

30. What is the mass (in grams) of 7.35 mol water?
    a. 10.7 g
    b. 18 g
    c. 132 g
    d. 180.6 g

31. Which of the following orbitals is the last to fill?
    a. 1s
    b. 3s
    c. 4p
    d. 6s

32. What is the name of the binary molecular compound NO_5?
    a. nitro pentoxide
    b. ammonium pentoxide
    c. nitrogen pentoxide
    d. pentnitrogen oxide

33. How many different types of tissue are there in the human body?
    a. four
    b. six
    c. eight
    d. ten

34. What is the name of the outermost layer of skin?
    a. dermis
    b. epidermis
    c. subcutaneous tissue
    d. hypodermis

35. Which hormone stimulates milk production in the breasts during lactation?
    a. norepinephrine
    b. antidiuretic hormone
    c. prolactin
    d. oxytocin

36. Which of the following structures has the lowest blood pressure?
    a. arteries
    b. arteriole
    c. venule
    d. vein

37. Which of the heart chambers is the most muscular?
    a. left atrium
    b. right atrium
    c. left ventricle
    d. right ventricle

38. Which part of the brain interprets sensory information?
    a. cerebrum
    b. hindbrain
    c. cerebellum
    d. medulla oblongata

39. Which of the following proteins is produced by cartilage?
    a. actin
    b. estrogen
    c. collagen
    d. myosin

40. Which component of the nervous system is responsible for lowering the heart rate?

    a. central nervous system
    b. sympathetic nervous system
    c. parasympathetic nervous system
    d. distal nervous system

Social Studies

Question1 refers to the following chart:

Group	Arrived in New World	Settled in
British Catholics	1632	Maryland
British Pilgrims	1620	Plymouth Colony, Massachusetts
British Puritans	1607	Virginia
British Quakers	1681	Pennsylvania
Dutch traders	1625	Manhattan Island
French traders	1608	Quebec

1. Which of the following conclusions can you draw, based on the information in the chart?

    a. Religious influences strongly affected the growth of the North American colonies.

    b. The French had large settlements in what became the eastern United States.

    c. The Dutch did not get a fair deal for the land they purchased.

    d. The Spanish were the first to settle in North America.

Question2 refers to the following passage:

    In 1917, Orville Wright wrote of the invention of the airplane:
"When my brother and I built and flew the first man-carrying flying machine, we thought that we were introducing into the world an invention which would make further wars practically impossible. That we were not alone in this thought is evidenced by the fact that the French Peace Society presented us with medals on account of our invention. We thought governments would realize the impossibility of winning by surprise attacks, and that no country would enter into war with another when it knew it would have to win by simply wearing out the enemy."

2. Which of the following statements do you think best expresses what the Wright brothers thought of World War I?

    a. "Ah, that splendid little war!"

    b. "How exciting to see airplanes extending fighting into the air!"

    c. "Using airplanes in war is unacceptable."

    d. "We would like to meet General Rickenbacker."

Question3 refers to the following passage:

> *In 1988, the federal government, as part of the Clean Air Act, began to monitor visibility in national parks and wilderness areas. Eleven years later, the Environmental Protection Agency set forth an attempt to improve the air quality in wilderness areas and national parks.*

3. Who of the following historical persons would NOT have applauded this effort?
    a. President Richard M. Nixon, who signed the act in 1970.
    b. Rachel Carson, early environmentalist and author of *Silent Spring*.
    c. President Theodore Roosevelt, who set aside land for public parks.
    d. the senator who campaigned in the early 1900s on the promise "Not one penny for scenery!"

Questions 4 and 5 refer to the following chart:

United States Foreign Trade 1960–1970
(by Category Percentages)

Category	1960		1970	
	Exports	Imports	Exports	Imports
Chemicals	8.7	5.3	9.0	3.6
Crude materials (except fuel)	13.7	18.3	10.8	8.3
Food and beverages, including tobacco	15.6	22.5	11.8	15.6
Machinery and transport	34.3	9.7	42.0	28.0
Mineral fuels and related materials	4.1	10.5	3.7	7.7

4. In 1960, which of the following categories had the greatest disparity between percentage of both exports and imports?
    a. chemicals
    b. crude materials
    c. food and beverages
    d. machinery and transport

5. Which category saw the greatest percentage decrease in imports between 1960 and 1970?

    a. chemicals
    b. crude materials
    c. food and beverages
    d. machinery and transport

Questions 6 and 7 refer to the following chart:

Per Capita National Debt

Year	Historical Context	Amount
1790	Following American Revolution at the beginning of the national government	$19
1816	After the War of 1812	$15
1866	Following the Civil War	$78
1919	After World War I	$240
1948	Three years after World War II ended	$1,720
1975	After the Vietnam War	$2,475
1989	Near the close of Reagan's administration	$11,545

6. Which of the following armed conflicts increased the per capita national debt by the largest *percentage* over the previous conflict listed?

    a. War of 1812
    b. Civil War
    c. World War I
    d. World War II

7. What does the change of per capita national debt between 1790 and 1816 likely indicate?

    a. The United States borrowed more money to pay for the War of 1812.
    b. The new nation worked hard to pay off debts owed from the Revolutionary War.
    c. People spent money very seldom between those wars.
    d. More citizens bought Treasury bonds in those days.

8. When the euro was introduced in January 2002, a single euro was valued at 88 cents in United States currency. In the summer of 2008, at one point it required $1.60 U.S. to buy 1 euro. In late October 2008, the euro fell to its lowest level against the dollar in two years. Which of the following statements represents an accurate conclusion?

    a. The world in 2008 was headed for another Great Depression.
    b. The dollar regained strength after significant devaluing against the euro.
    c. The euro remains the world's strongest currency.
    d. Investors need to keep buying stocks.

Questions 9 and 10 refer to the following chart:

Revenue Sources: 2004

Source	Amount in Millions	Percentage of Budget
Corporation income taxes	$189.3	10.1
Excise [sales] taxes	$69.9	3.7
Individual income taxes	$809.0	43.0
Social insurance and retirement receipts	$733.4	39.0
Other	$78.4	4.2

9. If the government were to end the use of offshore tax havens for corporations, as President Barack Obama promised in his 2008 campaign, how would the chart change?

    a. Corporate income taxes would decrease.

    b. Retirement receipts would increase.

    c. Individuals would pay less in income taxes.

    d. The share of corporate income taxes would increase.

10. Which category of taxpayer contributes the most to the federal budget?

    a. individuals

    b. corporations

    c. businesses paying Social Security tax

    d. federal government agencies

Questions 11 and 13 refer to the following map:

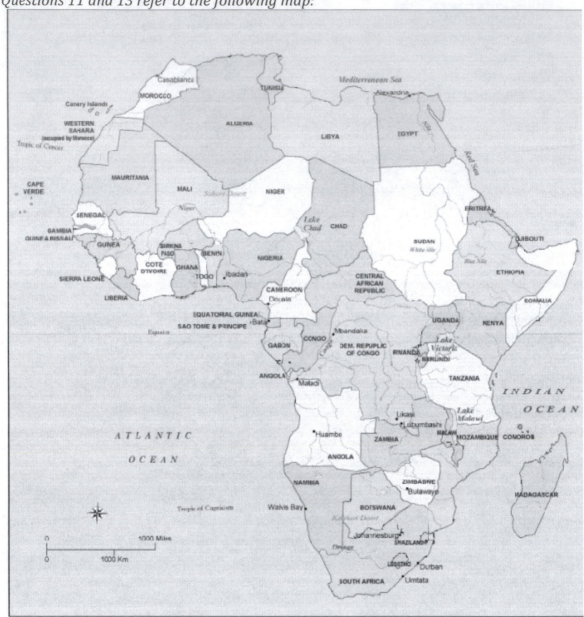

11. In Sudan, the Nile River splits into which bodies of water?
    a. Gulf of Aden and Red Sea
    b. Congo River and Lake Chad
    c. Lake Victoria and the White Nile
    d. The Blue Nile and the White Nile

12. What major geographical feature is located in Botswana?
    a. Zambezi River
    b. Lake Tanganyika
    c. Kalahari Desert
    d. Congo River

13. Which of the following countries is NOT located along the Indian Ocean?
    a. Cameroon
    b. Somalia
    c. Mozambique
    d. Kenya

14. Which of the following statements is not correct concerning feminism in the 1970s and 1980s?
    a. President Ronald Reagan appointed Sandra Day O'Connor as the first female Supreme Court justice.
    b. The administration of Republican President Ronald Reagan was generally against feminist goals.
    c. The Equal Rights Amendment, which supported the goals of feminism, was passed by Congress in 1972.
    d. The Equal Rights Amendment was ratified by Congress in 1983.

15. Which of the following statements regarding immigration to America during the 1980s is not true?
    a. Twice as many immigrants came to America during the 1980s than during the 1970s.
    b. Latin Americans comprised the largest proportion of immigrants to America in the 1980s.
    c. Most immigrants to the US in the 1980s were Latin American, Asian, and Caribbean.
    d. The 1986 Immigration Reform and Control Act impeded illegal Mexican immigration.

16. Of the following factors, which is not true regarding the US presidential election of 1992?
    a. George Bush's handling of the Persian Gulf War earned him high approval ratings.
    b. Bill Clinton received 47% of the votes while George Bush received 35% of votes.
    c. Problems with America's domestic economy worked against Bush in the election.
    d. Bill Clinton's campaign platform as a less liberal Democrat helped him in the race.

17. Which of the following statements regarding laws passed during the Clinton administration to control crime is not correct?
    a. The Brady Handgun Violence Prevention Act stipulated a five-day waiting period to buy a handgun.
    b. Following the shooting and consequent disability of James Brady, the "Brady Bill" passed without opposition.
    c. The Brady Handgun Violence Prevention Act allocated funds for a background-checking computer system.
    d. In 1994, Congress passed Clinton's bill to fund 100 000 additional police officer hires with over $8 billion.

18. Which of the following statements regarding the 1998 impeachment of President Clinton is not correct?
    a. The grounds for impeachment were perjury and obstruction of justice.
    b. The House of Representatives voted for the impeachment of Clinton.
    c. The Senate voted to impeach before Clinton was acquitted of charges.
    d. Clinton first denied a relationship with Lewinsky, and then admitted to it.

19. Which of the following statements is not true regarding the events of September 11, 2001, in the US?
    a. Shortly after that date the US defeated the Taliban and captured Al-Qaeda leader Osama bin Laden.
    b. On September 11, 2001, Muslim terrorists flew two hijacked airplanes into the World Trade Center in New York.
    c. On September 11, 2001, Muslim terrorists flew a hijacked passenger airliner into the Pentagon in Arlington, Virginia.
    d. An airplane hijacked by Muslim terrorists crashed in Pennsylvania after passengers resisted the terrorists.

20. What was the earliest written language in Mesopotamia?
    a. Sumerian
    b. Elamite
    c. Akkadian
    d. Aramaic

21. During which of these periods were pyramids not built in Egypt?
    a. The Old Kingdom
    b. The Middle Kingdom
    c. The New Kingdom
    d. The Third Dynasty

22. Which statement is not true regarding ancient Greek democracy?
    a. Democracy began to develop approximately 500 B.C.E.
    b. One of the first, best-known democracies was in Athens
    c. It was a direct democracy, not using any representatives
    d. It was a democracy completely open to all of the public

23. Which of the following choices most recently controlled a majority of India?
    a. The Gupta Dynasty
    b. The Maurya Empire
    c. The Mughal Empire
    d. The Maratha Empire

24. Which of the following are not included in a geographical definition of Southeast Asia?
    a. Myanmar, Laos, Cambodia, and Thailand
    b. Vietnam, the Malay Peninsula, and Brunei
    c. East Malaysia, Indonesia, and the Philippines
    d. These are all geographical parts of Southeast Asia

25. The current definition of the term "Latin America" is most correctly described as:
    a. Everywhere in the Americas that Spanish or Portuguese predominantly is spoken
    b. Everywhere in the Americas south of the United States, including the Caribbean
    c. Everywhere in the Americas where a Latinate (i.e. Romance) language is spoken
    d. All of the previous choices can correctly describe a current definition of the term "Latin America"

26. Which of the following statements correctly identifies the source of the term "Indians" for Native American peoples?
    a. It is a translation of a tribal word meaning "people of the land"
    b. It is a variation of the term "aborigine" that changed over time
    c. It refers to the fact that these people first migrated from India
    d. It refers to Columbus' erroneous thinking that he found the West Indies

27. Which of the following is not true about Democracy and the formation of the United States?

    a. The founding fathers stated in the Constitution that the USA would be a democracy

    b. The Declaration of Independence did not dictate democracy but stated its principles

    c. The United States Constitution stipulated that government be elected by the people

    d. The United States Constitution had terms to protect some, but not all, of the people

28. Who wrote about the concept of the Social Contract, which was incorporated into the Declaration of Independence?

    a. None of these

    b. All of these

    c. Thomas Hobbes

    d. John Locke

29. Historian Richard B. Morris identified seven men among the many identified as Founding Fathers of the United States who were most important in forming our nation. These seven included George Washington, Thomas Jefferson, and Benjamin Franklin. Whom of the following did he not include in the rest of the seven?

    a. Patrick Henry

    b. John Adams

    c. John Jay

    d. James Madison

30. Which of the following statements is not true about slavery in America?

    a. The Spanish brought African slaves to Florida by in the 1560s

    b. Chattel (ownership) slavery was legal in America from 1654 to1865

    c. Indentured servants preceded slaves in America as sources of labor

    d. Southern colonies imported more slaves in the 1600s to farm cotton

31. Which of the following is not true about the United States Constitution?

    a. It is the oldest written constitution still used by any country today

    b. Its first thirteen amendments make up the Bill of Rights document

    c. It is the shortest written constitution still used by any nation today

    d. It replaced the Articles of Confederation after a period of six years

32. Which of the following statements is correct regarding U. S. political parties?

    a. Democrat and Republican have been the two main parties since 1787

    b. The Democratic Party was first established in 1854

    c. The Republican Party was first established in 1824

    d. None of these statements is correct regarding U. S. political parties

33. Which of the following statements related to the annexation of Texas to the U.S.A. is incorrect?
a. Texas declared its independence from Mexico in 1836
b. Texas asked to join the Union after the Texas Revolution
c. Texas' addition was supported by President James Polk
d. Texas was invited to join the Union before asking to join

34. In 20th-century America, which of the following occurred first?
a. The Emergency Quota Act was passed by Congress
b. European immigration peaked at almost 1.3 million
c. Congress passed a very restrictive Immigration Act
d. The Great Depression caused decreased immigration

35. Which of the following statements about immigration to the United States from 2000-2005 is incorrect?
a. Less immigration to the United States occurred in these years than in other years
b. More immigration to the United States occurred in these years than in other years
c. There was greater border security in the United States after the 9/11 attacks
d. Almost eight million persons immigrated to the U.S. at this time

36. Which of these statements about Africa is true?
a. It is nearly twice the size of the continental United States.
b. It includes about 20 percent of the world's land surface but only 12 percent of its population.
c. Almost the entire continent lies south of the equator.
d. Nearly 50 percent of southern Africa consists of rain forest.

37. Which of these presidents most greatly expanded the power of the presidency?
a. Thomas Jefferson
b. Herbert Hoover
c. Lyndon Johnson
d. George W. Bush

38. The physical geography of a region most directly affects:
a. the religious beliefs of the native population.
b. the family structure of the native population.
c. the dietary preferences of the native population.
d. the language spoken by the native population.

39. A nation that is NOT a member of NAFTA is:
    a. Mexico.
    b. Brazil.
    c. the United States.
    d. Canada.

40. The main reason that the Federal Reserve Board lowers interest rates is to:
    a. lower prices.
    b. stimulate consumer spending.
    c. encourage international trade.
    d. control inflation.

Answers and Explanations

English

1. B: The passage refers to the nameless shoemaker's haggard eyes, his inability to focus on a question, his repetitive motions, and his inability to give his name. There is no indication of any art or gallery. The setting is Paris; the passage does not indicate that. Thus choice A is incorrect. The man being described is not identified as British or as a member of government, so choice C is incorrect. The man is making shoes, not hospital calls; therefore, choice D is incorrect. Although the man is making shoes by hand, there is no sign that he is a fashion designer.

2. A: The man gives his name as One Hundred and Five, North Tower, an address, not a personal name. The reference to a tower suggests a prison. Option B is an incorrect choice; the man has not apparently been out of the North Tower in many years. Nor is option C correct because the man is not precisely homeless. Nothing in the passage tells the reader when the man left home, so option D can be eliminated.

3. D: The man does not laugh in this passage. Choice A is clearly stated in the passage. He has lapses in conversation with Mr. Lorry. It is also clear in the passage that the man has no remembrance of a given personal name, so choice B can be eliminated. The repeated motion of his hands when they do not hold the shoe is a telling sign of derangement, so choice C is incorrect.

4. D: The man is working on a lady's walking-shoe when his visitors arrive and states that he had learned the trade, which was not his original manner of work, at his own request since arriving at the prison. He even expresses some pride in the quality of his work, which is based on a pattern because he has never seen the current mode of shoe. There is no indication that he is engaged in carving wood, blowing glass, smiting, or dressmaking. All of the other choices are clearly false.

5. B: Defarge is somehow the man's keeper and is concerned with his well-being. The first choice suggests unkindness, which is clearly not the case—Defarge is neutral at best. That option can be eliminated. He does not appear to be a family member, so choice C can be eliminated as well. These is also no suggestion of cruelty nor of a profession nor of a definite setting, leaving choice D untenable. A man in this setting is unlikely to have any money.

6. C: The lines that indicate this is correct are those referring to her surely forgiving him, his honest remorse, and determination to be a new man.

7. A: Adjectives reinforcing this idea include *quiet, shady, pleasant, white, cool,* and *sweet*. The second choice cannot be supported by the text; there is no indication of a

storm or wind. The sea and its waves are absent from the passage, eliminating choice C. Response D is not clearly stated in the text; we do not read of anything indicative of changes about to occur.

8. D: He refers to his need for forgiveness and desire to make a new life. The fact that his wife is going by her maiden name indicates a repudiation of her marriage. Marion, who is referred to as "the woman who had been his wife" greets him impersonally, and Gerta looks adoringly at Marion, not at him. Choice A is incorrect; no other children are present to indicate an orphanage. The disdainful reaction of the women indicates that this child is not his wife's, eliminating option B. Nothing in the text suggests that the child is unwell, making choice C wrong.

9. B: The flowers that the man sees in the parlor remind him of his former happiness and the love he has lost. Marion's decision to use her maiden name would not bring the man happiness. Thus choice A is incorrect. Madonna is a word for mother, which Marion was not; the word describes Gerta, making choice C wrong. The wide doorway is not linked to his former happiness, making the fourth option wrong.

10. C: Support for this is found in the text, which includes the sentence "Marion, calm, steady, definitely impersonal, nothing but a clear pallor to hint of inner stress." The words *pale* and *pallor* are related. The first response is incorrect; the text does not indicate a fear of seeing him alone. The second response also is false; Marion does not refuse to see him. She speaks no kind words to him, however, making choice four incorrect.

11. C: Choice C is the best answer. The sentence reads, "Your brain <u>filters</u> [your nose] out," which means your brain ignores it.

12. B: Only choice B reflects the meaning of the term "retina," which is a part of the eye's anatomy.

13. B: The final sentence reads, "Your brain works hard to make the world look continuous." It follows that visual perception is an active process, not a passive one, making choice B the best answer.

14. A: If the reader follows the instructions given in the paragraph, the O and X in the middle of the passage can be used to demonstrate the blind spot in the visual field. Choice A is the best answer.

15. B: The passage explains the way that visual perception works. Choice B is the best answer.

16. D: Much of the information in the passage is provided to show examples of how the brain fills in gaps in the visual field. Choice D is the best answer.

17. A: The author of the passage mentions the nose to demonstrate how the brain filters information out of the visual field. Choice A is the best answer.

18. B: Choice B can be inferred from the second paragraph. The paragraph states that the brain filters out information, which means that the brain does not perceive all activity in the visual field.

19. C: The passage states that a pluralistic society means one that embraces "many points of view," which is closest in meaning to choice C, "tolerant."

20. B: This passage does not choose one point of view on the issue, so only choice B is in keeping with the passage's purpose, which is to explain the disagreements between the earliest political parties in the US.

21. B: The word <u>competitive</u> means that the country would be able to compete financially with other countries. Choice B, stronger, is the best choice.

22. B: The passage explains the conflicting interests these two political parties represent. Choice B best reflects that point.

23. A: <u>It</u> refers to the noun "identity." Choice A is the best choice.

24. B: Since the passage does not choose to argue a particular point of view, the best choice would be the most neutral statement, choice B.

25. D: Choice D best reflects the true position of the Federalist Party.

26. A: Choice A best represents the Democratic-Republican Party's perspective.

27. B: The final paragraph mentions the Civil War only to show that these differing perspectives would not be easily reconciled. Choice B is the best answer.

28. C: The longest word recorded in an English dictionary are "Pneumonoultramicroscopicsilicovolcanokoniosis."
Error: Subject-verb disagreement
The subject of this sentence is the singular noun "word," so the plural verb "are" disagrees with the subject. The verb used here should be the singular "is."

29. B: The largest catfish ever catch is 646 pounds, the size of an adult brown bear.
Error: *Incorrect verb tense*
The verb "catch" is not in the appropriate tense. It should be written in the past tense, "caught."

30. C: Though a highly influentially anthropologist, Claude Levi-Strauss often took criticism for spending little time in the field studying real cultures.
Error: *Adverb / adjective error*

The adverb "influentially" is being used to modify the noun "anthropologist." Since adverbs cannot modify nouns, "influentially" should be written in adjective form: "influential."

31. C: It is easy to get confused when calculating time differences between time zones a useful way to remember them is that the Atlantic Ocean starts with A, as in A.M., and the Pacific Ocean starts with P, as in P.M.

Error: *Run-on sentence*

Choice C contains two complete thoughts, each with its own subject and predicate. The second complete thought begins, "a useful way to remember them…." A sentence composed of two complete thoughts joined together without appropriate punctuation is called a "run-on." A period or semicolon should appear between the phrases "time zones" and "a useful way."

32. D: No error.

33. C: "Graitful" should be spelled "grateful."

34. C: "Sower" should be spelled "sour."

35. B: "Sinator" should be spelled "senator."

36. A: The sentence, "<u>Many people have proposed explanations for this drop</u>," provides an introduction to the short explanations that follow. It should come after the first sentence.

37. B: The third sentence of this passage refers to "these insecticides," but there is no earlier reference to any insecticides in the paragraph. The sentence, "Insects that carry the disease can develop resistance to the chemicals, or insecticides, that are used to kill the mosquitoes," needs to be placed after sentence 2 for sentence 3 to make sense.

38. A: All of the sentences except sentence A contain errors. Sentences B and C contain verb errors; sentence D is a run-on sentence.

39. B: All of the sentences except sentence B contain verb errors.

40. A: Sentence A contains no errors. Sentence B is less clear than sentence A because it is awkwardly written in the passive voice. Sentence C contains a subject-verb agreement error. Sentence C switches pronouns from "We" to "I" in mid-sentence.

Mathematics

1. D: Integers include all positive and negative whole numbers and the number zero. The product of three integers must be an integer, so you can eliminate any answer choice that is not a whole number: choices (A) and (C). The product of two even integers is even. The product of even and odd integers is even. The only even choice is 24.

2. A: If $520 \div x = 40n$, then
$$(40n)(x) = 520 \text{ or}$$
$$40nx = 520$$
$$nx = 13.$$

3. D: Angles around a point add up to 360 degrees. Add the degrees of the given angles: $72° + 110° + 58° = 240°$. Then subtract from $360° - 240° = 120°$. Remember to divide $120°$ in half, since the question is asking for the degree measure of one angle, angle d.

4. B: Translate this word problem into a mathematical equation. Let Janice's weight = x. Let Elaina's weight = $x + 23$. Let June's weight = $x + 14$. Add their weights together and subtract 25 pounds:
$$= x + x + 23 + x + 14 - 25$$
$$= 3x + 37 - 25$$
$$= 3x + 12.$$

5. B: Add the 14 blue, 6 red, 12 green and 8 purple buttons to get a total of 40 buttons. If 25 buttons are removed, there are 15 buttons remaining in the bag. If the chance of drawing a red button is now 1/3, divide 15 into thirds to get 5 red buttons remaining in the bag. The original total of red buttons was 6; so $6 - 5 = 1$: one red button was removed, choice (B).

6. C: Divide the mg the child should receive by the number of mg in 0.8 ml to determine how many 0.8 ml doses the child should receive: $240 \div 80 = 3$. Multiply the number of doses by 0.8 to determine how many ml the child should receive: $3 \times 0.8 = 2.4$ ml

7. D: This equation is asking you to multiply three algebraic expressions. When multiplying more than two expressions, multiply any two expressions (using the foil method), then multiply the result by the third expression. Start by multiplying:
$(y + 1)(y + 2) = (y \times y) + (y \times 2) + (1 \times y) + (1 \times 2)$
$= y^2 + 2y + y + 2$
$= y^2 + 3y + 2$
Then multiply the result by the third expression:
$(y^2 + 3y + 2)(y + 3) = (y^2 + 3y + 2)(y) + (y^2 + 3y + 2)(3)$

$= (y^3 + 3y^2 + 2y) + (3y^2 + 9y + 6)$
$= y^3 + 3y^2 + 2y + 3y^2 + 9y + 6$
$= y^3 + 3y^2 + 3y^2 + 9y + 2y + 6$
$= y^3 + 6y^2 + 11y + 6$

8. D: The area of a parallelogram is base X height or $A = bh$, where b is the length of a side and h is the length of an altitude to that side. In this problem, $A = 6 \times 4$; $A = 24$. Remember, use the length of BE, not the length of CD for the height.

9. A: There are a total of 90 students that take Math, English, or both. You must avoid counting the same students twice, and you may find it helpful to create a Venn diagram or some sort of chart to keep the different types of students separate.

Total students	90
Students taking both courses:	-50
Students taking just English:	-25
Students taking just Math: =	15

10. A: To find the interest earned, multiply the interest rate by the deposit amount. Because this account uses simple interest, you do not need to worry about compounding the interest. Remember to convert the interest rate to a percentage. $0.0375 \times 2,500 = 93.75$.

Choice (D) might be a tempting answer, since it is the deposit amount added to the interest earned, but the question asks how much interest will be earned, not the total amount of the deposit after earning interest.

11. C: To solve this problem, first calculate how many gallons each toilet uses in 375 flushes:
$3.2 \times 375 = 1,200$ gallons
$1.6 \times 375 = 600$ gallons
The problem is asking for the difference, so find the difference between the regular toilet and the low-flow toilet:
$1,200 - 600 = 600$ gallons. Note that you could also find the difference in water use for one flush, and then multiply that amount by 375:
$3.2 - 1.6 = 1.6$
$1.6 \times 375 = 600$.

12. D: Use the formula for probability to solve this problem:
Probability = <u>Number of Desirable Outcomes</u>
                      Number of Possible Outcomes

Because there are effectively multiple events – the roll of each die is its own event – you must multiply all the possible outcomes for each die. Thus, to determine the number of possible outcomes, multiply the number of sides on dice exponentially by the number dice:

$6^5 = (6 \times 6 \times 6 \times 6 \times 6) = 7{,}776$
There is one desirable outcome: rolling all sixes. Probability = $^1/_{7{,}776}$

13. B: Remember to use the order of operations when simplifying this equation. The acronym *PEMDAS* will help you remember the correct order: Parenthesis, Exponentiation, Multiplication/Division, Addition/Subtraction.
$4(6 - 3)^2 - (-2)$
First, simplify the parentheses: $4 \times 3^2 - (-2)$
Next, simplify the exponent: $4 \times 9 - (-2)$
Then multiply: $36 - (-2)$
Finally, subtract: $36 - (-2) = 36 + 2 = 38$
The PEMDAS method is used to simplify multiple equations in this practice test.

14. B: Angles that form a straight line add up to 180 degrees. Such angles are sometimes referred to as being "supplementary."
$60 + 2x = 180$
$2x = 120$
$x = 60$

15. A: You can eliminate choices (B) and (C) since they are to the left of the decimal point. This problem asks for the number in the thousandths place, and the "ths" indicate digits to the right of the decimal point. Of those digits:

- 9 is in the tenths place.

- 7 is in the hundredths place.

- 3 is in the thousandths place.

- 8 is in the ten thousandths place.

16. D: To solve for n, you have to isolate that variable by putting all of the other terms of the equation, including coefficients, integers, and variables on the other side of the equal sign.
Add p to each side of the equation:
$4n - p = 3r$
$4n - p (+ p) = 3r (+ p)$
$4n = 3r + p$
Divide each term by 4:
$4n/4 = n = 3r/4 + p/4$

17. D: An equilateral triangle has three sides of equal length. If each side is 4 inches long, the perimeter of the triangle is 12 inches. A square has four sides of equal length. Since its perimeter also must equal 12 inches, divide 12 by 4: $12 \div 4 = 3$,

18. A: The sum of the measures of the angels in a triangle equals 180°. Use the numbers given in the figure to make the following equation:

$6x + 8x + 4x = 180$

$18x = 180$

$x = 10$

19. D: Use the formula for circumference:

Circumference = π X diameter (π is approximately equal to 3.14).

To give the best estimate, round to the nearest whole number:

3.14 rounds to 3

12.2, the diameter, rounds to 12

3 x 12 = 36

20. A: The average of a group of terms is the sum of the terms divided by the number of terms.

To solve this word problem, let x = Paula's fourth test score.

$$\frac{88 + 84 + 91 + x}{4} = 90$$

$$\frac{263 + x}{4} = 90$$

$263 + x = 360$

$x = 97$

21. D: Turn the word problem into an equation. Remember that product means multiplication: 4^2 X 6 = 96.

22. C: This equation is asking you to multiply three algebraic expressions. When multiplying more than two expressions, multiply any two expressions, (using the FOIL method) then multiply the result by the third expression. Start by multiplying:

$(y + 2)(y + 3) = (y \text{ X } y) + (y \text{ X } 3) + (2 \text{ X } y) + (2 \text{ X } 3)$

$= y^2 + 3y + 2y + 6$

$= y^2 + 5y + 6$

Then multiply the result by the third expression:

$(y^2 + 5y + 6)(y + 4) = (y^2 + 5y + 6)(y) + (y^2 + 5y + 6)(4)$

$= (y^3 + 5y^2 + 6y) + (4y^2 + 20y + 24)$

$= y^3 + 5y^2 + 6y + 4y^2 + 20y + 24$

$= y^3 + 9y^2 + 26y + 24$

23. B: One side of a square is 56cm. All of its sides are equal, and the perimeter is the sum of all sides.

Therefore, the perimeter equals 56cm+56cm+56cm+56cm

The perimeter is 224cm

24. B: $5 \times (80 / 8) + (7 - 2) - (9 \times 5) =$
Remember the order of operations: Parentheses, exponents, multiplication, division, addition, subtraction.
Perform the operations inside the parentheses first:
$5 \times (10) + (5) - (45) =$
Then, do any multiplication and division, working from left to right:
$50 + 5 - 45 =$
Finally, do any adding or subtracting, working from left to right:
$55 - 45 = 10$

25. A: Since we know the value of x and y, it is simply a matter of substituting them into the expression:
$9x - 3y + 8xy - 3$
$9(10) - 3(-2) + 8(10)(-2) - 3$
$90 + 6 - 160 - 3$
$96 - 163 = -67$

26. B: $9x (3x^2 + 2x - 9)$
To simplify, multiply the value outside of the brackets $(9x)$ by the values inside of the brackets.
$9x \cdot 3x^2 + 9x \cdot 2x - 9x \cdot 9$
$27x^3 + 18 x^2 - 81x$

27. D: $x^5 x^2 + y^0 =$
We know that $x = 3$.
Therefore, we can find the value of $x^5 x^2$
$3^5 3^2$
$243 \cdot 9 = 2,187$
Any value to the power of zero is equal to one.
Therefore, $2,187 + 1 = 2,188$

28. C: y represents the number of students who bought a used textbook. Each used textbook cost $50. Therefore, to figure out the total amount spent on used textbooks, the number of students who bought one would have to be multiplied by 50.
Algebraically, this can be represented by $50y$.

29. D: $-4x + 8 \geq 48$
To solve for x, first isolate the variable.
$-4x \geq 48 - 8$
$-4x \geq 40$
Then, divide both sides by -4 to solve for x.

When an inequality is divided by a negative number, the sign must change directions.

$-4x/-4 \geq 40/-4$

$x \leq -10$

30. B: $x^2 + 12x + 36 = 0$

To solve for x, this equation must be factored.

$(x + 6)(x + 6)$

Then, solve for x.

$x + 6 = 0$

$x = -6$

31. B: $\dfrac{64x^4 + 8x^3 - 4x^2 + 16x}{8x}$

To simplify, each term in the numerator can be divided by $8x$ to eliminate the denominator. When variables with an exponent are divided by one another, the exponent in the denominator is subtracted from the exponent in the numerator. We are left with: $8x^3 + x^2 - x/2 + 2$

32. C: $9x^2y - 18xy - 27y$

$9y$ is contained in all parts of this expression. Therefore, $9y$ can be factored out.

$9y(x^2 - 2x - 3)$

$(x^2 - 2x - 3)$ can also be factored.

$(x - 3)(x + 1)$

We end up with $9y(x - 3)(x + 1)$

33. A: $\sqrt{3}(5\sqrt{3} - \sqrt{12} + \sqrt{10})$

To simplify, all terms inside the brackets must be multiplied by $\sqrt{3}$

$5\sqrt{3} \times \sqrt{3} - \sqrt{3} \times \sqrt{12} + \sqrt{10} \times \sqrt{3}$

$5\sqrt{9} - \sqrt{36} + \sqrt{30}$

Since the square root of 9 and 36 are whole numbers, this expression can be further simplified.

$5 \times 3 - 6 + \sqrt{30}$

$15 - 6 + \sqrt{30}$

$9 + \sqrt{30}$

34. C: $25x - 12x + 6x - 27 = 35$

To make solving easier, combine like terms.

$19x = 35+27$

$19x = 62$

$x = 62 \div 19$

$x = 3.26$

35. D: $(y + 10)^2 - 625 = 0$
First, move the 625 to the other side of the equation.
$(y + 10)^2 = 625$
Then, take the square root of both sides.
$\sqrt{(y + 10)^2} = \sqrt{625}$
$\sqrt{(y + 10)^2} = \pm 25$
$y+10 = 25$ and $y+10 = -25$
Then, it is simply a matter of solving for y
$y + 10 = 25$, so $y = 25 - 10 = 15$
and
$y + 10 = -25$, so $y = -25 - 10 = -35$

36. A: $2x - 6y = 12$
$-6x + 14y = 42$
To solve a variable using a system of equations, one of the variables must be cancelled out. To eliminate x from these equations, first multiply the top equation by 3.
$3(2x - 6y = 12)$
$6x - 18y = 36$
Then, add the two equations to eliminate x.

$$\begin{array}{r} 6x - 18y = 36 \\ +\ \underline{-6x + 14y = 42} \\ -4y = 78 \end{array}$$

Solve for y.
$-4y = 78$
$y = 78/-4$
$y = -19.5$

37. A: Use the first equation to solve for x.
$6x + 2x - 26 = -5x$
$8x + 5x = 26$
$13x = 26$
$x = 2$
Then, evaluate the second equation.
$[(2x - 1)/7]^3$
$[(2 \times 2-1)/7]^3$
$[3/7]^3$
$[0.4285]^3$
$= 0.0787$

38. B: To calculate the slope of a line, we simply have to figure out the change in y over the change in x.

$\underline{18 - 2}$
-3 - 5

$\underline{16} = -2$
 -8

-2 is the slope of the line.

39. C: Lines that are perpendicular to each other have negative reciprocal slopes. The slope of the original equation is $-5x$.

The negative reciprocal of this is $x/5$. The value of the y-intercept is not important for the purpose of answering this question.

40. D: To find a midpoint, simply calculate the average of the two sets of points.
For x, the midpoint is calculated in the following manner:
$(-20 + 5)/2 = -7.5$
For y, the midpoint is calculated in the following manner:
$(8 + 3)/2 = 5.5$
The midpoint is (-7.5, 5.5)

Science

1. A: The peak for albumin is the highest in the electropherogram, so the concentration of albumin is higher than that of any other component. Answers B-D are incorrect, since all the corresponding peaks are lower.

2. D: The peak for component γ is furthest from the origin along the mobility axis, indicating that it has moved the furthest during the experiment. Answers A-C are incorrect, since the corresponding peaks are further to the left, indicating lesser mobility for these components.

3. C: The peak for component α1 lies to the right of that for albumin, indicating greater mobility, and to the right of all the other peaks, indicating lesser mobility than the components represented by those peaks. Since small molecules move faster than large ones, α1 must be smaller than albumin and larger than the other components.
Answer A is incorrect because the peak for α1 is to the right (faster) than albumin and to the left (slower) than the others.
Answer B is incorrect because the peak for α1 is to the right (smaller) than albumin and to the left (larger) than the others.
Answer D is incorrect because the data say nothing about whether or not the component is a protein.

4. D: The peak for component γ is the fastest, indicating that γ is the smallest component seen on the electropherogram.
Answers A-C are incorrect because all these components move more slowly than component γ.

5. D: The peak for the unknown lies between those for γ and β, indicating an intermediate size. It has moved more rapidly than all components except for component γ.
Answers A and B are incorrect, because the unknown is smaller than β.
Answer C is incorrect, because the unknown is faster than most of the others.

6. D: If the unknown is an aggregate, it must be larger than the components that have clumped together to form it, not smaller. Answers A-C are incorrect, because the components they refer to are all larger than the unknown, so they cannot form it by aggregation.

7. D: If the unknown is a breakdown product, it must be smaller than the components that have broken down to form it, not larger. Answers A-C are incorrect, because the components they refer to are all larger than the unknown, so it _may_ be true that any of these have formed it by breaking down.

8. D: The experiment shows only that this patient's blood contains an unknown component. It does not demonstrate that the component causes the patient's disease, or that it results from it. It may be unrelated. Further experiments are required to fully characterize the relationship between the component and the illness.

Answers A-C are incorrect because all assume a cause-and-effect relationship between the component and the patient's illness, but this has not been demonstrated by this one experiment.

9. A: As stated in the text, the size of each circle is proportional to the number of recoveries.

10. D: The graph shows that the largest number of circles, and the largest circles as well, are at this depth. Since the size of the circles is proportional to the number of fish recovered, the greatest numbers of these fish were at these depths.

11. C: 2011 fish were recovered out of 34,000 released. The percentage is given by
$$P = 100 \times \frac{2,011}{34,000} = 6\%.$$

12. B: The median age at each depth is shown by the X symbols on the plot. For this depth, the symbol lines up approximately with the mark corresponding to 5 years on the upper axis of the graph.

13. D: Although not specifically described in the text, all of the reasons stated may occur, reducing the recovery of tagged fish. The conclusions of the study must assume that the fraction of fish recovered (sample) are representative of the population as a whole.

14. D: The chart describes the age of the fish, but does not provide any information concerning their size.

15. B: The median age of the populations recovered at each depth is shown by the X symbol on the plot, and corresponds to progressively older fish at greater depths. Although some of the other statements are true, they are not supported by the data in the figure.

16. C: The right-most symbol on the plot shows that some 20-year old fish were recovered at depths of 501-700 meters. No older fish were recovered in this study.

17. B: Oxygen is not one of the products of the Krebs cycle. The *Krebs cycle* is the second stage of cellular respiration. In this stage, a sequence of reactions converts pyruvic acid into carbon dioxide. This stage of cellular respiration produces the phosphate compounds that provide most of the energy for the cell. The Krebs cycle is also known as the citric acid cycle or the tricarboxylic acid cycle.

18. C: The sugar and phosphate in DNA are connected by covalent bonds. A *covalent bond* is formed when atoms share electrons. It is very common for atoms to share pairs of electrons. An *ionic bond* is created when one or more electrons are transferred between atoms. *Ionic bonds*, also known as *electrovalent bonds*, are formed between ions with opposite charges. There is no such thing as an *overt bond* in chemistry.

19. A: The second part of an organism's scientific name is its species. The system of naming species is called binomial nomenclature. The first name is the *genus*, and the second name is the *species*. In binomial nomenclature, species is the most specific designation. This system enables the same name to be used all around the world, so that scientists can communicate with one another. Genus and species are just two of the categories in biological classification, otherwise known as taxonomy. The levels of classification, from most general to most specific, are kingdom, phylum, class, order, family, genus, and species. As you can see, binomial nomenclature only includes the two most specific categories.

20. B: Unlike other organic molecules, lipids are not water soluble. Lipids are typically composed of carbon and hydrogen. Three common types of lipid are fats, waxes, and oils. Indeed, lipids usually feel oily when you touch them. All living cells are primarily composed of lipids, carbohydrates, and proteins. Some examples of fats are lard, corn oil, and butter. Some examples of waxes are beeswax and carnauba wax. Some examples of steroids are cholesterol and ergosterol.

21. D: *Hemoglobin* is not a steroid. It is a protein that helps to move oxygen from the lungs to the various body tissues. Steroids can be either synthetic chemicals used to reduce swelling and inflammation or sex hormones produced by the body. *Cholesterol* is the most abundant steroid in the human body. It is necessary for the creation of bile, though it can be dangerous if the levels in the body become too high. *Estrogen* is a female steroid produced by the ovaries (in females), testes (in males), placenta, and adrenal cortex. It contributes to adolescent sexual development, menstruation, mood, lactation, and aging. *Testosterone* is the main hormone produced by the testes; it is responsible for the development of adult male sex characteristics.

22. A: The property of cohesion is responsible for the passage of water through a plant. *Cohesion* is the attractive force between two molecules of the same substance. The water in the roots of the plant is drawn upward into the stem, leaves, and flowers by the presence of other water molecules. *Adhesion* is the attractive force between molecules of different substances. *Osmosis* is a process in which water diffuses through a selectively permeable membrane. *Evaporation* is the conversion of water from a liquid to a gas.

23. C: *Melatonin* is produced by the pineal gland. One of the primary functions of melatonin is regulation of the circadian cycle, which is the rhythm of sleep and wakefulness. *Insulin* helps regulate the amount of glucose in the blood. Without insulin, the body is unable to convert blood sugar into energy. *Testosterone* is the main hormone produced by the testes; it is responsible for the development of adult male sex characteristics. *Epinephrine*, also known as adrenaline, performs a number of functions: It quickens and strengthens the heartbeat and dilates the bronchioles. Epinephrine is one of the hormones secreted when the body senses danger.

24. C: *Ribosomes* are the organelles that organize protein synthesis. A ribosome, composed of RNA and protein, is a tiny structure responsible for putting proteins together. The *mitochondrion* converts chemical energy into a form that is more useful for the functions of the cell. The *nucleus* is the central structure of the cell. It contains the DNA and administrates the functions of the cell. The *vacuole* is a cell organelle in which useful materials (for example, carbohydrates, salts, water, and proteins) are stored.

25. A: Boron does not exist as a diatomic molecule. The other possible answer choices, fluorine, oxygen, and nitrogen, all exist as diatomic molecules. A diatomic molecule always appears in nature as a pair: The word *diatomic* means "having two atoms." With the exception of astatine, all of the halogens are diatomic. Chemistry students often use the mnemonic BrINClHOF (pronounced "brinkelhoff") to remember all of the diatomic elements: bromine, iodine, nitrogen, chlorine, hydrogen, oxygen, and fluorine. Note that not all of these diatomic elements are halogens.

26. D: Hydriodic acid is another name for aqueous HI. In an aqueous solution, the solvent is water. Hydriodic acid is a polyatomic ion, meaning that it is composed of two or more elements. When this solution has an increased amount of oxygen, the -*ate* suffix on the first word is converted to -*ic*. This process can be quite complex, so you should carefully review this material before your exam.

27. C: CH could be an empirical formula. An empirical formula is the smallest expression of a chemical formula. To be empirical, a formula must be incapable of being reduced. For this reason, answer choices A, B, and D are incorrect, as they could all be reduced to a simpler form. Note that empirical formulas are not the same as compounds, which do not have to be irreducible. Two compounds can have the same empirical formula but different molecular formulas. The molecular formula is the actual number of atoms in the molecule.

28. A: A limiting reactant is entirely used up by the chemical reaction. Limiting reactants control the extent of the reaction and determine the quantity of the product. A reducing agent is a substance that reduces the amount of another substance by losing electrons. A reagent is any substance used in a chemical reaction. Some of the most common reagents in the laboratory are sodium

hydroxide and hydrochloric acid. The behavior and properties of these substances are known, so they can be effectively used to produce predictable reactions in an experiment.

29. B: The horizontal rows of the periodic table are called periods. The vertical columns of the periodic table are known as groups or families. All of the elements in a group have similar properties. The relationships between the elements in each period are similar as you move from left to right. The periodic table was developed by Dmitri Mendeleev to organize the known elements according to their similarities. New elements can be added to the periodic table without necessitating a redesign.

30. C: The mass of 7.35 mol water is 132 grams. You should be able to find the mass of various chemical compounds when you are given the number of mols. The information required to perform this function is included on the periodic table. To solve this problem, find the molecular mass of water by finding the respective weights of hydrogen and oxygen. Remember that water contains two hydrogen molecules and one oxygen molecule. The molecular mass of hydrogen is roughly 1, and the molecular mass of oxygen is roughly 16. A molecule of water, then, has approximately 18 grams of mass. Multiply this by 7.35 mol, and you will obtain the answer 132.3, which is closest to answer choice C.

31. D: Of these orbitals, the last to fill is 6s. Orbitals fill in the following order: 1s, 2s, 2p, 3s, 3p, 4s, 3d, 4p, 5s, 4d, 5p, 6s, 4f, 5d, 6p, 7s, 5f, 6d, and 7p. The number is the orbital number, and the letter is the sublevel identification. Sublevel s has one orbital and can hold a maximum of two electrons. Sublevel p has three orbitals and can hold a maximum of six electrons. Sublevel d has five orbitals and can hold a maximum of 10 electrons. Sublevel f has seven orbitals and can hold a maximum of 14 electrons.

32. C: Nitrogen pentoxide is the name of the binary molecular compound NO_5. The format given in answer choice C is appropriate when dealing with two nonmetals. A prefix is used to denote the number of atoms of each element. Note that when there are seven atoms of a given element, the prefix *hepta-* is used instead of the usual *septa-*. Also, when the first atom in this kind of binary molecular compound is single, it does not need to be given the prefix *mono-*.

33. A: There are four different types of tissue in the human body: epithelial, connective, muscle, and nerve. *Epithelial* tissue lines the internal and external surfaces of the body. It is like a sheet, consisting of squamous, cuboidal, and columnar cells. They can expand and contract, like on the inner lining of the bladder. *Connective* tissue provides the structure of the body, as well as the links between various body parts. Tendons, ligaments, cartilage, and bone are all examples of connective tissue. *Muscle* tissue is composed of tiny fibers, which contract to move the skeleton. There are three types of muscle tissue: smooth, cardiac, and skeletal.

Nerve tissue makes up the nervous system; it is composed of nerve cells, nerve fibers, neuroglia, and dendrites.

34. B: The epidermis is the outermost layer of skin. The thickness of this layer of skin varies over different parts of the body. For instance, the epidermis on the eyelids is very thin, while the epidermis over the soles of the feet is much thicker. The dermis lies directly beneath the epidermis. It is composed of collagen, elastic tissue, and reticular fibers. Beneath the dermis lies the subcutaneous tissue, which consists of fat, blood vessels, and nerves. The subcutaneous tissue contributes to the regulation of body temperature. The hypodermis is the layer of cells underneath the dermis; it is generally considered to be a part of the subcutaneous tissue.

35. C: *Prolactin* stimulates the production of breast milk during lactation. *Norepinephrine* is a hormone and neurotransmitter secreted by the adrenal gland that regulates heart rate, blood pressure, and blood sugar. *Antidiuretic hormone* is produced by the hypothalamus and secreted by the pituitary gland. It regulates the concentration of urine and triggers the contractions of the arteries and capillaries. *Oxytocin* is a hormone secreted by the pituitary gland that makes it easier to eject milk from the breast and manages the contractions of the uterus during labor.

36. D: Of the given structures, veins have the lowest blood pressure. *Veins* carry oxygen-poor blood from the outlying parts of the body to the heart. An *artery* carries oxygen-rich blood from the heart to the peripheral parts of the body. An *arteriole* extends from an artery to a capillary. A *venule* is a tiny vein that extends from a capillary to a larger vein.

37. C: Of the four heart chambers, the left ventricle is the most muscular. When it contracts, it pushes blood out to the organs and extremities of the body. The right ventricle pushes blood into the lungs. The atria, on the other hand, receive blood from the outlying parts of the body and transport it into the ventricles. The basic process works as follows: Oxygen-poor blood fills the right atrium and is pumped into the right ventricle, from which it is pumped into the pulmonary artery and on to the lungs. In the lungs, this blood is oxygenated. The blood then reenters the heart at the left atrium, which when full pumps into the left ventricle. When the left ventricle is full, blood is pushed into the aorta and on to the organs and extremities of the body.

38. A: The *cerebrum* is the part of the brain that interprets sensory information. It is the largest part of the brain. The cerebrum is divided into two hemispheres, connected by a thin band of tissue called the corpus callosum. The *cerebellum* is positioned at the back of the head, between the brain stem and the cerebrum. It controls both voluntary and involuntary movements. The *medulla oblongata* forms the base of the brain. This part of the brain is responsible for blood flow and breathing, among other things.

39. C: *Collagen* is the protein produced by cartilage. Bone, tendon, and cartilage are all mainly composed of collagen. *Actin* and *myosin* are the proteins responsible for muscle contractions. Actin makes up the thinner fibers in muscle tissue, while myosin makes up the thicker fibers. Myosin is the most numerous cell protein in human muscle. *Estrogen* is one of the steroid hormones produced mainly by the ovaries. Estrogen motivates the menstrual cycle and the development of female sex characteristics.

40. C: The parasympathetic nervous system is responsible for lowering the heart rate. It slows down the heart rate, dilates the blood vessels, and increases the secretions of the digestive system. The central nervous system is composed of the brain and the spinal cord. The sympathetic nervous system is a part of the autonomic nervous system; its role is to oppose the actions taken by the parasympathetic nervous system. So, the sympathetic nervous system accelerates the heart, contracts the blood vessels, and decreases the secretions of the digestive system.

Social Studies

1. A: Catholics, Pilgrims, Puritans, and Quakers all were instrumental in developing new colonies, allowing one to deduce the importance of religion. Answer 2 is incorrect because the French did not hold a great deal of territory in the eastern United States but in regions west of the Appalachians and in what became Canada. Response 3 is incorrect; although there is nothing on the chart to confirm this information, the low price of Manhattan is a well-known story. Answer 4 is also true, but that information cannot be discerned from the chart.

2. C: The men had expected their invention to end war; instead, it became a new weapon. Response 1 is often cited as a reference to the Spanish-American War of 1898. Thus it is incorrect. The Wright brothers, hoping that their invention would put an end to war, would likely not express the idea in response 2. Rickenbacker was a famous World War I ace pilot, but given the Wright brothers' desires for peace and their own fame, they probably would not be interested in meeting him. Thus response 4 is incorrect.

3. D: A politician who did not want to allocate even a penny for "scenery" would likely not have favored the Clean Air Act. All others would have favored the measures. Response 1 is not the right answer because Nixon signed the bill; in 1970, he was still a popular president, so he did not need to sign to create goodwill. Rachel Carson, who sounded an early warning about the effects of DDT, would likely have been thrilled with the act. Theodore Roosevelt was a strong supporter of environmental causes and would have championed the bill. Muir was a great lover of wild places and no doubt would have been delighted with the act's passage.

4. D: Machinery and transport jumped from 34.3 to 42.0 percent in exports and from 9.7 to 28.0 percent in imports. Chemicals increased exports slightly, from 8.7 to 9.0. Imports declined slightly, from 5.3 to 3.6. Thus answer 1 is incorrect. Crude material exports declined from 13.7 to 10.8 while imports declined from 18.3 to 8.3, making response 2 incorrect. The decline in exports of food and beverages was just under 4 percent while imports declined 7 percent, so answer 3 is not an accurate choice. Exports of mineral fuels and related materials declined less than a full percentage point while imports declined nearly 3 points.

5. B: Crude material imports declined by 10 percentage points. All other categories saw imports that declined less than 10 points over the decade. Chemicals decreased in that time by only 1.7 percent, making response 1 inaccurate. Answer 3 is also incorrect; food and beverages decreased during those ten years by just over 7 percent. Imports of machinery and transport nearly tripled, rather than decreased, which means response 4 is incorrect. Mineral fuels and related materials declined by nearly 3 percentage point.

6. C: Following World War I, the per capita national debt increased by 32 percent over that of the Civil War. Answer 1 is not an accurate choice; the amount of debt per capita actually decreased between the American Revolution and the War of 1812. Between the War of 1812 and the Civil War, the percentage of debt increased by almost 14 percent, so answer number 2 is also incorrect. The per capita national debt increased after World War I by nearly 14 percent, making answer 4 wrong as well. After the Vietnam War, the percentage increased by 21 percent.

7. B: The only time that the national debt level fell after a war was after the American Revolution. The conclusion drawn is that the new government felt an obligation to demonstrate fiscal responsibility to the world. Answer 1 is incorrect; borrowing more money would increase the debt, not lower it. Response 3 is not correct. The amount of money people spent had nothing to do with the per capita national debt. Purchase of Treasury bonds would indicate a growing debt, which was the opposite of the actual case, making answer 4 incorrect.

8. B: Although the nation faced recession, the U.S. dollar made a comeback in world currency during the fall of 2008. Response 1 cannot be concluded from the information given, which focuses solely on the dollar and euro rather than on the entire world. Response 3 is incorrect as well; the euro fell in 2008 against the dollar. The wisdom of buying stocks cannot be concluded from the information given; therefore, option 4 is not viable.

9. D: Corporate taxes would be paid in greater amounts because businesses would no longer be able to shelter offshore. Response 1, which suggests the opposite situation, is clearly incorrect. The offshore tax havens have nothing to do with retirement receipts, so option 2 is also incorrect. Again, individual income tax is not related to the problem of offshore tax havens, making response 3 incorrect as well.

10. A: Individuals provide the largest segment of the total revenue sources, 43 percent. Response 2 is incorrect; corporations, because of legal loopholes, were contributing only 10.1 percent of the revenue in 2004. Social Security is included as part of the 39 percent of the amount that comes from social insurance and retirement receipts, making answer 3 not accurate. Likewise, answer 4 is wrong; government agencies do not pay taxes and do not appear on the chart.

11. D: At Khartoum, which is Sudan's capital, the Nile splits into the White and Blue Nile rivers. Response 1 is not accurate; the Gulf of Aden is north of Somalia, as is the Red Sea. Response 2 is incorrect; neither the Congo River nor Lake Chad is in Sudan, nor does either of them come from the Nile. The third answer is not correct because Lake Victoria is not in Sudan at all but farther south.

12. C: The Kalahari Desert is located in the middle western part of Botswana. Choice 1 is not correct; the Zambezi River runs through Zambia and Angola, countries that are north of Botswana. The second answer is also wrong; Lake Tanganyika is

northeast of Botswana, along Tanzania's western border. The Congo River is in the Democratic Republic of the Congo, also located north of Botswana, making choice 4 not correct.

13. A: Cameroon is on the Atlantic coast, south of Nigeria and north of Gabon. Choice 2 is not accurate. Somalia is bordered by both the Indian Ocean and the Gulf of Aden; its capital, Mogadishu, is right on the Indian Ocean. Answer 3 is incorrect; Mozambique, near the southern part of the continent, is bordered by the Indian Ocean. Answer 4, Kenya, near the middle of the African continent, likewise, is an inaccurate choice. Kenya is also bordered by the Indian Ocean. Like the others, Tanzania is along the Indian Ocean, south of Kenya.

14. D: The Equal Rights Amendment, though it was approved by Congress in 1972 (c), was not ratified in its deadline year for ratification of 1983, is not correct. The amendment fell short of reaching ratification by just three states' votes. President Reagan did appoint judge Sandra Day O'Connor, the first female justice, to the Supreme Court (a), despite the fact that in general, he and his administration were against feminist agendas (b).

15. D: The statement that the 1986 Immigration Reform and Control Act impeded illegal Mexican immigration is not true. This legislation punished employers with sanctions for hiring undocumented employees, but despite this the illegal immigration of Mexicans to America was largely unaffected by the law. It is true that twice as many people immigrated to America in the 1980s than in the 1970s (a): the number reached over nine million in the 80s. It is true that the majority of immigrants were Latin American (b). In addition to Latin Americans, other large groups of immigrants in the 1980s were Asians and Caribbean inhabitants (c).

16. B: Bill Clinton did not receive 47% of the votes but 43.2%, while George Bush received not 35% but 37.7% of the votes. In other words, this was a close election. Although Bush's actions to resolve the Persian Gulf War did earn him high public approval ratings (a), problems with the economy in America weakened his bid for reelection (c). Arkansas Governor Bill Clinton's campaign focusing on his views as a more moderate, less liberal, Democrat appealed to voters (d). Another factor that detracted from Bush's campaign was the third-party candidacy of H. Ross Perot, a billionaire businessman from

17. B: The "Brady Bill" passed without opposition, is not correct. When John Hinckley Jr. tried to assassinate President Reagan in1981, he failed, but he severely wounded James Brady, Reagan's Press Secretary, who was riding with him. Brady almost died and suffered permanent disabilities. When the Brady Handgun Violence Prevention Act (1993) was proposed, the National Rifle Association (NRA) lobbied vigorously against it. However, Congress passed the bill over this powerful group's objections. This law mandated a five-day waiting period before a person could buy a handgun (a) and allocated funds towards the design of a computer system that

could more quickly and efficiently run background checks (c). Additional crime control legislation proposed by the Clinton administration included a 1994 bill that allocated more than $8 billion to hire an additional 100 000 police officers (d).

18. C: The Senate never voted to impeach Clinton. The grounds for impeachment were perjury and obstruction of justice (a) based upon Clinton's denial of an extramarital relationship with intern Monica Lewinsky. Clinton later admitted to the relationship (d). The House of Representatives voted to impeach the President (b) under the influence of Speaker of the House Newt Gingrich and other Republicans. After a trial in the Senate, the Senate voted against convicting Clinton, and he was acquitted of all charges. As this represented a defeat to the Republicans, Newt Gingrich resigned shortly thereafter. Many people agreed with First Lady Hillary Clinton that the entire impeachment episode, regardless of Clinton's actions, was part of a "vast right-wing conspiracy" against Clinton by Republicans, which she stated had gone on since he announced his candidacy for President.

19. A: It is not true that the US defeated the Taliban and captured Osama bin Laden shortly after 9/11/2001. Osama bin Laden was killed during a raid on a private compound in Pakistan in 2011, nearly 10 years after the attacks. It is true that Muslim terrorists flew two of the four American airplanes they had hijacked into the twin towers of the World Trade Center in New York City (b). They flew the third of the four planes into the US Department of Defense's headquarters, the Pentagon building in Arlington, Virginia, (c) near Washington, D.C. The fourth plane crashed in a field near Shanksville, Pennsylvania, after some of the passengers on board tried to overtake the terrorists (d). President George W. Bush announced a "war on terrorism" after these attacks killed a total of 2,995 people.

20. A: The earliest written language in Mesopotamia was Sumerian. Ancient Sumerians began writing this language around 3500 B.C.E. Elamite (b), from Iran, was the language spoken by the ancient Elamites and was the official language of the Persian Empire from the 6th to 4th centuries B.C.E. Written Linear Elamite was used for a very short time in the late 3rd century B.C.E. The written Elamite cuneiform, used from about 2500 to 331 B.C.E., was an adaptation of the Akkadian (c) cuneiform. Akkadian is the earliest found Semitic language. Written Akkadian cuneiform first appeared in texts by circa 2800 B.C.E., and full Akkadian texts appeared by circa 2500 B.C.E. The Akkadian cuneiform writing system is ultimately a derivative of the ancient Sumerian cuneiform writing system, although these two spoken languages were not related linguistically. Aramaic (d) is another Semitic language, but unlike Akkadian, Aramaic is not now extinct. Old Aramaic, the written language of the Old Testament and the spoken language used by Jesus Christ, was current from c. 1100-200 C.E. Middle Aramaic, used from 200-1200 C.E., included literary Syriac (Christian groups developed the writing system of Syriac in order to be able to write spoken Aramaic) and was the written language of the Jewish books of Biblical commentary (Namely, the Talmud, the Targum, and the Midrash). Modern Aramaic has been used from 1200 to the present. Hurrian was the language

spoken and written by the Hurrians or Khurrites, a people who migrated into Northern Mesopotamia, from circa 2300-1000 B.C.E. They are thought to have emigrated from Armenia, settled in Syria, and spread through Southeast Anatolia and Northern Mesopotamia, thereby establishing the Mitanni Kingdom in Northern Mesopotamia during that time period.

21. C: The New Kingdom was the period during which no more pyramids were built in Egypt. The Pyramids were built between the years of 2630 and 1814 B.C.E., and the New Kingdom spanned from circa 1550-1070 B.C. As a result, the last pyramid was built approximately 264 years before the New Kingdom began. 2630 B.C.E. marked the beginning of the reign of the first Pharaoh, Djoser, who had the first pyramid built at Saqqara. 1814 B.C.E. marked the end of the reign of the last Pharaoh, Amenemhat III, who had the last pyramid built at Hawara. In between these years, a succession of pharaohs built many pyramids. The Old Kingdom (a) encompasses both the Third (d) and Fourth Dynasties; therefore, all three of these choices encompass pyramid-building periods. Djoser's had his first pyramid built during the Third Dynasty (d). The Pharaohs Kufu, Khafre, and Menkaure, respectively, build the famous Pyramids of Giza during the Fourth Dynasty (e) during their reigns at different times between circa 2575 and 2467 B.C.E., the period of the Fourth Dynasty. The Middle Kingdom (b) encompassed the 11th through 14th Dynasties, from circa. 2080 to 1640 B.C.E.—also within the time period (2630-1814 B.C.E.) when pyramids were built by the Pharaohs.

22. D: Ancient Greek democracy was not completely open to all of the public. However, participating persons were not chosen or excluded based on their respective socioeconomic levels. The city-state of Athens had one of the first and most well-known democracies in ancient Greece (b). It began around 500 B.C.E. (a). The experiment of Athenian democracy was unique in that it was a direct democracy, meaning people voted directly for or against proposed legislation without any representation (c) such as the House of Representatives and the Senate, as we have in modern democracies.

23. D: The Maratha Empire or Maratha Confederacy controlled a majority of India in the middle of the 18th century. In chronological order, the Maurya Empire (b) ruled India in the 3rd century B.C.E., prospering under the command of Ashoka the Great. The Gupta Dynasty (a) ruled India beginning in the 3rd century C.E. (i.e. 600 years after the Maurya Empire). The Gupta Dynasty presided over ancient India's "Golden Age." After a number of invasions coming from the steppes of central Asia between the 10th and 12th centuries, the Delhi Sultanate came to dominate a majority of northern India, circa 1206-1526. The Mughal Empire (c) ruled this area after the Delhi Sultanate, from 1526 to the middle of the 19th century.

24. D: These are all geographically parts of Southeast Asia. The countries of Myanmar (Burma), Laos, Cambodia, and Thailand (a) are considered Mainland Southeast Asia, as are Vietnam and the Malay Peninsula (b). Brunei (b), East

Malaysia, Indonesia, and the Philippines (c) are considered Maritime Southeast Asia, as are Singapore and Timor-Leste (d). The Seven Sister States of India (d) are also considered to be part of Southeast Asia, geographically and culturally. (The Seven Sister States of India are Arunachal Pradesh, Assam, Nagaland, Meghalaya, Manipur, Tripura, and Mizoram, which all have contiguous borders in northeastern India.)

25. D: All of these can correctly describe a current definition of the term Latin America because more than one definition of this name can be used. One definition is (a) everywhere in the Americas where Spanish or Portuguese is predominantly spoken; i.e., Mexico, most of Central America and South America, Cuba, the Dominican Republic, and Puerto Rico. This definition is based on the colonial history of the Spanish and Portuguese Empires. A second definition is (b) everywhere in the Americas south of the United States, including the Caribbean. By this definition, many English-speaking countries, such as Jamaica, the Bahamas, Trinidad and Tobago, etc. would be included, as would French-speaking countries such as Haiti, Martinique, Guadeloupe, and French Guiana. This definition places more emphasis on socioeconomic colonial history than on culture. To clarify and avoid what seems an overly simplistic name, the United Nations refers instead to "Latin America and the Caribbean" to define this area. A third definition currently used is (c) everywhere in the Americas where a Latinate (i.e. Latin-based or Romance) language is spoken. This includes Spanish, Portuguese, and French. (Note: Romanian is also a Romance language, but many people tend to forget this.) Although French is spoken in Québec, nobody refers to it as part of Latin America because it is considered such an integral part of Canada. In this definition, anywhere creole languages based on Spanish, Portuguese, or French are spoken also is included.

26. D: The most correct identification of the source of the term "Indians" for Native Americans is: Columbus, while searching for a water route to Asia, stumbled upon the Americas but thought he had landed in the West Indies. As a result, he called the natives "Indians" and the name became a tradition. "Indian" is neither a translation of a tribal word (a) nor a variation of the word aborigine (b). "Aborigine" is a synonym with "indigenous" but is not related to the term "Indian" It does not refer to Native Americans having originally migrated from India (c); instead, the predominant theory asserts that they migrated from Eurasia.

27. A: It is not true that the founding fathers specifically stated in the Constitution that the USA would be a democracy. The founding fathers wanted the new United States to be founded on principles of liberty and equality, but they did not specifically describe these principles with the term "Democracy." Thus, the Declaration of Independence, like the Constitution after it, did not stipulate a democracy, although both did state the principles of equality and freedom (b). The Constitution also provided for the election of the new government (c), and for protection of the rights of some, but not all, of the people (d). Notable exceptions at the time were black people and women. Only later were laws passed to protect their rights over the years.

28. B: All of these wrote about the idea of a Social Contract between government and the people that was used in the Declaration of Independence as a democratic principle. Thomas Hobbes (c) wrote about it in his Leviathan (1651), describing it in the context of an authoritarian monarchy. John Locke (d) wrote about it in his Second Treatise of Government (1689), describing it in the context of a liberal monarchy. Jean-Jacques Rousseau wrote about it in his Du Contrat Social, or The Social Contract (1762), in the context of a liberal republic similar to what the new USA would become. These works supplied a theoretical basis for constitutional monarchies, liberal democracies, and republicanism. Since answer (b), all of these, is correct, answer (a), none of these, is incorrect.

29. A: Patrick Henry was not included in Morris' list of seven (Seven Who Shaped Our Destiny: The Founding Fathers as Revolutionaries, 1973). Henry, often remembered for his famous quotation "Give me liberty or give me death!" had more interest in and placed more value on state politics than national politics. He was chosen as a Virginia delegate to the Constitutional Convention, but he did not attend. Morris' list does include John Adams (b), John Jay (c), James Madison (d), and Alexander Hamilton. All of these men attended the Convention in 1776 and signed the Declaration of Independence. (In addition to attending and signing, George Washington presided over the Convention.)

30. D: It is not true that cotton farming was the reason Southern colonies imported more slaves in the 1600s. Tobacco farming was the reason. Tobacco became a very successful cash crop at that time in the American colonies. Growing tobacco was extremely labor-intensive, so planters needed more slaves as tobacco became more popular and valuable. Cotton was grown in America by the end of the 16th century and increased around the end of the 18th century due to Eli Whitney's invention of the cotton gin in 1793. However, during the Civil War, the Union blockaded Southern ports, and the Confederacy restricted exports of cotton to Britain as an economic strategy, hoping to force Britain either to acknowledge the Confederacy or to become involved in the war. Without American cotton, Britain and France, its two biggest consumers, turned to Egypt for their cotton imports. Thus, cotton was not the biggest cash crop during the Civil War. Instead, tobacco was the South's biggest cash crop through the 17th and 18th centuries until cotton replaced it in the middle of the 19th century. It is true that slaves were brought from Africa to Florida by the Spanish as early as the 1560s (a), although this practice became more widespread practice in the 1600s. Chattel slavery (meaning outright ownership of a slave for the slave's lifetime) was legal in America from 1654 until 1865 (b) when Lincoln's Emancipation Proclamation abolished it. Furthermore, indentured servants provided sources of labor in America before slaves (c). These servants were both black and white people who were bonded into servitude for a period of several years, after which they could gain their freedom. The labor of indentured servants helped to pay for transportation of people to the colonies from Europe or other lands. An eventual shortage of indentured servants led to the importation of slaves.

By the 18th century, court rulings had confined American slavery to mostly African or African-American people.

31. B: It is not true about the U.S. Constitution that its first thirteen amendments make up the Bill of Rights. The Bill of Rights consists of the first TEN amendments to the Constitution. Furthermore, the United States Constitution is actually both the oldest (a) and the shortest (c) written constitution still used by any country in the world today. The Constitution replaced the Articles of Confederation after a period of six years (d). The Articles of Confederation were ratified in 1781, and the Constitution was ratified in 1787.

32. D: None of these statements is correct regarding U.S. political parties. The Democratic and Republican Parties have not been the two main parties since 1787 (a); instead, these parties have been the two main parties since the General Election of 1856. 1787 was the year that the U. S. Constitution was ratified. The Democratic Party was not founded in 1854 (b) but in 1824. The Republican Party was not founded in 1824 (c) but in 1854. It is not correct that no third-party candidate has been President since the Civil War. Instead, Theodore ("Teddy") Roosevelt ran as the Progressive Party's candidate in 1912, won 20% of the popular vote, and was elected President.

33. D: The incorrect statement is that Texas was invited to join the Union before asking to join. The annexation of Texas was controversial because Texas was a slave state. Texas did declare its independence from Mexico in 1836 (a). This was the era of Manifest Destiny, so many expansionists favored annexation. However, Presidents Andrew Jackson and Martin van Buren both declined Texas' request to join the Union (b), in large part because they feared the issue of slavery would split the Democratic Party. Before the 1844 election, both Henry Clay, the Whig candidate, and the expected Democratic candidate, previous President Martin van Buren, opposed annexation as they did not want it to become a campaign issue. Nevertheless, James K. Polk was in favor of annexing Texas (c), and the Democratic Party unexpectedly chose him as their candidate instead of van Buren. After Polk won the election but before he took office, Congress approved Texas' annexation.

34. B: The first event was immigration of Europeans to America hit a high in 1907, when 1,285,349 European immigrants came to America. The numbers were so great that Congress passed the Emergency Quota Act (a) in 1921. In order to implement greater restrictions on the influx of Southern and Eastern Europeans—particularly Jews, Italians, and Slavs—arriving in larger numbers since the 1890s, and even more as refugees before and during the Nazi and World War II years, Congress further passed the 1924 Immigration Act (c), which prohibited most European refugees from entering the United States. During the Great Depression (d) of the 1930s, immigration declined sharply due to the lack of economic opportunities. The Immigration and Nationality Act Amendments of 1965, or the Hart-Cellar Act,

allowed a great many people from countries other than those in Europe to immigrate to America, thereby altering America's ethnic composition.

35. A: There was not less immigration to the U.S. from 2000-2005 than in other years. In fact, more immigration to the U.S. occurred in these five years than in any other five-year period of U.S. history (b). It is true that borders were more secure following the terrorist attacks of 9/11/2001 (c). However, despite increased security measures, almost eight million people immigrated to the U.S. (d), and of these numbers, nearly half entered the country illegally

36. B: Three times the size of the continental United States, Africa contains a surprisingly small percentage of the world population. The continent is divided roughly in half by the equator. The rain forest makes up about 15 percent of central Africa.

37. C: Johnson exerted his presidential power to advance the Great Society agenda and to enact major civil rights legislation. He also conducted a war in Vietnam without Congressional declaration. Jefferson, Hoover, and Bush were all outspoken advocates of limiting the role of government, including the executive branch.

38. C: Physical geography focuses on processes and patterns in the natural environment. What people eat in any given geographic region is largely dependent on such environmental factors as climate and the availability of arable land. Religion, family, and language may all be affected by geographical factors, but they are not as immediately affected as dietary preferences.

39. B: The North American Free Trade Agreement was established in 1994 by the United States, Canada, and Mexico in an effort to minimize trade barriers among the continent's three nations.

40. B: Lower interest rates allow banks to lend out more money, which serves to stimulate consumer spending. Increased spending tends to raise, not lower, prices. The Federal Reserve Board is not actively involved in international trade. The fear of inflation usually leads to a raise in interest rates.